Cambridge Elements

Elements in World Englishes
edited by
Edgar W. Schneider
University of Regensburg

OPTIMIZING DECISION TREES FOR THE ANALYSIS OF WORLD ENGLISHES AND SOCIOLINGUISTIC DATA

Sarah Buschfeld
TU Dortmund University

Claus Weihs
TU Dortmund University

Shaftesbury Road, Cambridge CB2 8EA, United Kingdom

One Liberty Plaza, 20th Floor, New York, NY 10006, USA

477 Williamstown Road, Port Melbourne, VIC 3207, Australia

314–321, 3rd Floor, Plot 3, Splendor Forum, Jasola District Centre,
New Delhi – 110025, India

Cambridge University Press is part of Cambridge University Press & Assessment, a department of the University of Cambridge.

We share the University's mission to contribute to society through the pursuit of education, learning and research at the highest international levels of excellence.

www.cambridge.org
Information on this title: www.cambridge.org/9781009470315
DOI: 10.1017/9781009470346

© Sarah Buschfeld and Claus Weihs 2026

This publication is in copyright. Subject to statutory exception and to the provisions of relevant collective licensing agreements, no reproduction of any part may take place without the written permission of Cambridge University Press & Assessment.

When citing this work, please include a reference to the DOI 10.1017/9781009470346

First published 2026

A catalogue record for this publication is available from the British Library

A Cataloging-in-Publication data record for this Element is available from the Library of Congress

ISBN 978-1-009-47031-5 Hardback
ISBN 978-1-009-47035-3 Paperback
ISSN 2633-3309 (online)
ISSN 2633-3295 (print)

Cambridge University Press & Assessment has no responsibility for the persistence or accuracy of URLs for external or third-party internet websites referred to in this publication and does not guarantee that any content on such websites is, or will remain, accurate or appropriate.

For EU product safety concerns, contact us at Calle de José Abascal, 56, 1°, 28003 Madrid, Spain, or email eugpsr@cambridge.org

Optimizing Decision Trees for the Analysis of World Englishes and Sociolinguistic Data

Elements in World Englishes

DOI: 10.1017/9781009470346
First published online: March 2026

Sarah Buschfeld
TU Dortmund University

Claus Weihs
TU Dortmund University

Author for correspondence: Sarah Buschfeld, sarah.buschfeld@tu-dortmund.de

Abstract: This Element introduces PrInDT (Prediction and Interpretation in Decision Trees), a statistical approach for modeling relationships between extra- and intralinguistic variables in World Englishes. It is based on decision trees and controls their size in a way that they are easy and straightforward to interpret. Furthermore, PrInDT optimizes their accuracy so that they best fit the data and can be reliably used for prediction. Moreover, it can handle unbalanced classes that occur, for example, when comparing non-standard with standard linguistic realizations. The various PrInDT functions can deal with classification and regression tasks and can analyze multiple endogenous variables jointly, even for models combining classification and regression. The authors introduce these features in some detail and apply them to World Englishes and sociolinguistic datasets. As examples, they draw on L1 child data from England and Singapore as well as linguistic landscapes data from the Eastern Caribbean island of St. Martin.

Keywords: statistics for linguists, modelling linguistic data, World Englishes, Sociolinguistics, variationist linguistics

© Sarah Buschfeld and Claus Weihs 2026

ISBNs: 9781009470315 (HB), 9781009470353 (PB), 9781009470346 (OC)
ISSNs: 2633-3309 (online), 2633-3295 (print)

Contents

1 Introduction — 1

2 Introducing the Data Sets — 3

3 Setting the Statistical Background — 12

4 PrInDT: Prediction and Interpretation of Decision Trees — 37

5 PrInDT Applications in World Englishes — 52

6 Achievements for World Englishes Studies — 90

7 Conclusion — 94

References — 96

1 Introduction

Early in the collaboration between the two authors of this Element, we identified a number of aspects that could be improved in the statistical analysis of linguistic data and World Englishes data in particular. These include the generalizability and interpretability of results, as well as model assessment. As a recent investigation has revealed (Buschfeld, Leuckert, et al. 2024), these aspects are often neglected in World Englishes studies. We therefore developed a new approach for statistical modeling that meets these shortcomings by generating interpretable decision trees, which are characterized by best possible model accuracy and whose results are not only based on the data sample under investigation but generalizable to a broader population. This new approach is presented in this Element in some detail and is compared to models commonly used in linguistic studies, in particular with respect to the generalizability and interpretability of results, as well as model evaluation. All the methods presented in the following are available in the so-called PrInDT package (Prediction and Interpretation in Decision Trees) in the software R (Weihs & Buschfeld 2025; R Core Team 2019).

In linguistics, statistical methods are widely used for analyzing data. The most prominent and frequently used textbooks on statistics for linguists are Rasinger (2013), which mainly relies on Excel, and Baayen (2008), Field et al. (2012), Levshina (2015), Schneider & Lauber (2020), Winter (2020), Gries (2021), and Sonderegger (2023), which focus on R. Statistical models typically used in linguistic analyses include various kinds of linear regression models (e.g., fixed effects, mixed effects) and logistic regression for classification (i.e., for categorical dependent variables). Linguists have also repeatedly made use of random forests and conditional inference trees (ctrees) and sometimes of Bayesian variants of statistical models (cf. Section 3). In Buschfeld, Leuckert, et al. (2024), we have shown that the actual use of statistical methods varies between linguistic subdisciplines and that the World Englishes paradigm slightly lags behind other subdisciplines in terms of frequency and sophistication of statistical approaches used.

A problem often related to the choice of the correct method and its sophistication is either scarcity of linguistic data (i.e., very low token frequencies of the variables of interest) or a high imbalance between large-class and small-class variants of the variable under investigation. In particular, linguists investigating sociolinguistic or regional variation of language, of which World Englishes scholars form a major part, are often confronted with this problem. They are commonly most interested in linguistic forms that diverge from the traditional standard variant of a language, and these forms often come with low frequencies or at least much lower frequencies than their standard variants. For example, if a linguistic nonstandard strategy such as the omission of subject pronouns or verbal inflections is supposed to be characteristic of a variety of English, it is often still not used by the majority of the population, in the majority of speech events. It is normally used interchangeably with the standard variant, depending on the speaker and communicative situation. Some very specific local characteristics, such as past-tense marking via *finish* as a postverbal marker in Singaporean English (cf. Section 2.1.3), are so rare that those statistical procedures often used in sociolinguistics or World Englishes, for example "simple" ctrees, would only predict the larger class – that is, the more frequent, often standard, variant. However, it is particularly the smaller, nonstandard class variationist linguists are most interested in, which is why it is important to make use of a statistical approach that adequately considers the smaller class, too.

The approach we developed and present in this Element builds on decision trees, which work on the basis of a series of relatively simple "if-then" rules based on priorly defined predictors. They are, therefore, easier to interpret than, for example, linear models, which use linear combinations of the predictors for modeling. To better understand the differences between the approaches and thus our decision in favor of decision trees, we also introduce linear models but ultimately focus on a particular kind of decision tree, namely conditional inference trees. For such trees, it is relatively easy to control their size and therefore their complexity and interpretability (cf. Sections 3.2.3.3 and 4.1). After the size of the tree is adjusted according to the given needs, we optimize model accuracy (cf. Sections 4.1 and 4.3). For the resulting model, we discuss the predictive behavior and the linguistic interpretation of the predictions (cf. Section 5.1). This way, we place the generalizability of the trees (i.e., the transferability of the results from the sample to the wider population) at the center of our discussion (cf. Section 4.1).

This Element does not aim to present novel linguistic studies or results, but instead focuses on PrInDT and its various applications. It draws on existing studies and data sets to illustrate the novel statistical methods and thus reads like a statistics manual more than a linguistic study. Following this introduction, Section 2 introduces the data sets and methods of the World Englishes case studies drawn upon for the various PrInDT applications. Section 3 describes and applies a number of standard statistical methods our PrInDT applications are based on, with which the reader should be familiar. This may, at times, be rather basic information for a statistical expert reader. However, we aim at a broad audience of readers and would like to give beginners in statistics a chance to follow our explanations and new approach, too. Ultimately, the new PrInDT methods are introduced in Section 4, before we apply them to World Englishes sample data in Section 5. For all analyses, we employ the software R and provide the relevant R-code. A brief, general introduction to R is presented in Section 3.1, while further explanations and applications can be found in the sections that follow. Section 6 summarizes the relevance of the new approach for the World Englishes paradigm, before we provide some overall conclusions in Section 7.

2 Introducing the Data Sets

Before we turn to the various applications of our approach (cf. Sections 4–6), we introduce the different data sets that have been used to develop the PrInDT approach, as well as some of its offspring versions and later advancements. The data were collected by the first author of the Element between 2014 and 2020. The PrInDT approach introduced in this Element was gradually developed, expanded, and modified between 2020 and 2025.

2.1 Data Sets I–IV: Investigating L1 Child Singaporean English

The first four data sets we introduce were collected for a large-scale research project investigating the acquisition of English as a first language (L1) in Singapore (Buschfeld 2020). Singaporean English (SingE) is one of the most extensively researched second-language (L2) varieties of English. However, for an ever-increasing number of children it is (one of) their home language(s). According to the *Straits Times*, one of the leading newspapers in Singapore, the number of students in primary school who speak mostly English at home has risen to around 70% in all three major ethnic groups in Singapore (i.e., the Chinese, Indian, and Malay; Chan 2020). This is clearly confirmed by recent census data, as the 2020 Census of Population in Singapore reports that in the group of 5 to 14 year olds, 77.4% of the Chinese, 63% of the Malay, and 69.8% of the Indian segments of the population nowadays speak English as the most frequently used language at home (Department of Statistics Singapore 2020: 29).

To place L1 SingE on the map of L1 varieties of English, Buschfeld (2020) has empirically and systematically investigated different linguistic characteristics of SingE, as well as the acquisitional route Singaporean children take in their linguistic development, and compared her findings to data collected from monolingual and bi-/multilingual children from England. In the following applications of the PrInDT approach, we make use of these data and investigate similar aspects of L1 SingE but base our investigation on a more sophisticated statistical approach.

The three features Buschfeld (2020) investigated in some detail (i.e., subject-pronoun realization, past-tense marking, and vowel-length realization) were chosen since earlier research has identified local realizations of them in SingE. The variables thus offer standard and nonstandard variants, whose realization, we hypothesize, is determined by different extra- as well as intralinguistic predictors, most importantly age, ethnicity, and linguistic background (cf. Sections 2.1.1–2.1.4 for a detailed introduction of the predictors). In this respect, we expect to find clear differences between children from England and Singapore, as they acquire English under quite different circumstances (i.e., in a traditional, officially monolingual English-speaking country versus a former L2 English setting). In the latter context, features like the omission of subject pronouns, SingE past-tense marking strategies, and potential mergers of long and short vowels are the products of general mechanisms of language acquisition, such as simplification strategies and L1 transfer from the local languages of Singapore (i.e., Chinese and Indian languages and Malay). This means that second-language learners – and this is what the Singaporean population originally was – take over linguistic characteristics of their L1 to their L2 (here English), even if they do not match the target grammar. This is how new varieties of English are born, be they L2 or ultimately L1 varieties in contexts such as Singapore. We provide further details on the collected data sets and examples of the local SingE realizations in the following sections (Sections 2.1.1, 2.1.3, and 2.1.4).

2.1.1 Subject-Pronoun Realization

First, we introduce the so-called *subpro* data set for the investigation of the realization of subject pronouns. The data were collected in Singapore and England in 2014 and 2015 and sourced from video-recorded task-directed dialogue between researcher and child, consisting of several parts: a grammar-elicitation task, a story-retelling task, elicited narratives, and free interaction. The data set includes subject-pronoun realizations of 30 male and female Singaporean children of different ethnicities, aged 2;5 (2 years, 5 months) to 12;1 (all multilingual), and 21 male and female children from England, aged 2;1 to 10;9 (multi- and monolingual). The recorded material was orthographically transcribed and manually coded for the realization of subject pronouns (*realized* versus *zero*, i.e., nonrealized). In all, we have 6,146 tokens of the subject-pronoun variable, whose realization can be interpreted by means of a detailed set of extra- and intralinguistic predictors introduced later in this section. A total of 528 subject pronouns were omitted and will thus be referred to as *zero* pronouns (for details on the exact methods of elicitation and data processing, cf. Buschfeld 2020: 90–94, 110–117).

The following examples illustrate some SingE variants of nonrealized subject pronouns (Buschfeld 2020: 144):

1. Researcher: ... What do you do with your friends? Do you play with them?
Child: [ØI] Play with them. Sometimes drawing....
Child: Sometimes [ØWE] play some fun things.
2. Child: I think in MH370, I think they can find because [ØIT] is easy to go there....

These and similar zero forms are variably used by children acquiring English as an L1 in Singapore. They are also typical of adult SingE and thus part of the input the children receive.

The aim of our analysis is to find prediction rules for the use of subject pronouns (*realized* versus *zero*) by means of extra- and intralinguistic variables. The extralinguistic variables considered as independent variables in the statistical analysis are ethnicity (ETH), age (AGE), sex (SEX), linguistic background (LiBa), and mean length of utterance (MLU). Mean length of utterance (MLU) is a measure that determines the syntactic complexity of utterances young children make and thus their grammatical development. It is an aggregated factor for which children were assigned to three groups according to the average grammatical complexity of 50 of their utterances. LiBa refers to the linguistic background of the children and splits the group into children who grow up with English only (mono) and multilingual children who acquire English and at least one further language (multi). The pronoun (PRN) is taken into account as an intralinguistic variable. Depending on the respective application, we work with pronoun categorization types of different granularity. We follow either the traditional distinction of three persons in singular and plural (i.e., *I*, *you*, *he*, *she*, *it*, *we*, *you*, *they*) – note, however, that plural tokens of *you* were not found in any of the data sets – or a distinction based on a more refined classification of *it*. In the most fine-grained classification of *it* (cf. Section 2.1.2), we differentiate the referential *it* ("This is my house. **It** is blue."), expletive *it* ("**It** is raining."), and a type Buschfeld (2020: 115–116) has labeled "contextual referential it." This notion roughly corresponds to what Halliday and Hasan (1976: 52–53) call "extended reference" or "text reference," as some uses of *it* show "a greater degree of referentiality" than others (e.g., "**It** was a perfect day," when the *it* refers to a priorly described event in general and not just a single noun phrase). Table 1 summarizes the variables, their levels, and the abbreviations used in the analysis of the *subpro* data.

In Sections 3.2.1, 3.2.3.2, 3.2.3.3, and 3.2.4, we analyze these data by means of classical statistical methods. In Sections 5.1 and 5.6, we apply our PrInDT approach to the data set to compare and discuss its potential advantages over the

Table 1 Subject pronouns: List of variables

Variable type	Variable	Levels	Abbreviation
Dependent	pronoun realization	realized, zero	class
Independent	pronoun	I, you_s (you singular), he, she, it, we, they	PRN
Independent	mean length of utterance	1, 2, 3, OL (outlier)	MLU
Independent	(ethnic) group	Singapore: Chinese, Indian, mixed (S/C, S/I, S/m) England: ancestral, migrant, mixed (E/a, E/migr, E/m)	ETH
Independent	age	in months of the individual child; numeric	AGE
Independent	sex	female, male	SEX
Independent	linguistic background	mono, multi, NA (not available)	LiBa

traditional approaches. The underlying methods of the PrInDT approach are introduced in Sections 4.5.1 and 4.5.6.

2.1.2 Subject-Pronoun Realization with an Unbalanced Predictor

In a second study based on the data set introduced in Section 2.1.1, we look into the realization of subject pronouns (*realized* or *zero*) in both L1 SingE and the L2 variety to carve out potential differences in language use between L1 and L2 speakers of English in Singapore. We report and discuss the results of the study by Weihs and Buschfeld (2021b), with slight modifications only, to complete the picture of how the underlying idea of PrInDT can be applied to various linguistic contexts and objectives.

This study compares the data introduced in Section 2.1.1 to data from the spoken part of the Singapore component of the International Corpus of English (ICE-Singapore). The subcorpus from Buschfeld's (2020) study amounts to 36,000 words. The ICE-data come from the 90 transcripts of approximately 2,000 words each in the spoken component > dialogues > private > face-to-face-conversations section. They comprise an overall total of 202,000 words from 254 adults (ages 18 and over). Since the ICE-data dates back to the early 1990s, the results might also lend themselves to an apparent time analysis of potentially ongoing language change in SingE.

The data from both sets were manually coded for the realization of subject pronouns. The corresponding data set is called *nessubpro*. All in all, 3,225 tokens were extracted from the child corpus (2,899 *realized*, 326 *zero*) and 17,325 tokens from the adult corpus (16,543 *realized*, 782 *zero*). Therefore, the data constitute a high imbalance not only in token frequencies between the small and the large classes (*zero* versus *realized*) but also between the child and adult tokens. We introduce how our PrInDT approach deals with this double imbalance in data sets in Section 4.5.2.

The aim of our analysis is to find prediction rules for the use of subject pronouns (*realized* versus *zero*) by means of extra- and intralinguistic variables similar to those introduced in Table 1 but extended by the level *adults* and different types of *it* (cf. Section 2.1.1).[1] Table 2 summarizes the variables, their levels, and the abbreviations used in the analysis. The imbalance between the child and adult tokens cannot be explicitly considered by classical statistical classification methods. Therefore, we only apply our PrInDT approach (cf. Section 4.5.2) to these data (cf. Section 5.2).

2.1.3 Past-Tense Marking

As a next sample study, we analyzed the child data introduced in Section 2.1.1 for the realization of past-tense morphology, again building and expanding on the study by Buschfeld (2020). As part of the overall data set, the grammatical elicitation task TEGI, or Test of Early Grammatical Impairment[2] (Rice & Wexler 2001), is specifically designed to elicit past-tense endings in young children (for details on the exact methods of elicitation and data processing; cf. Buschfeld 2020: 90–94; 117–120). The data set is called *past*. Examples 1 and 2 illustrate SingE options to indicate past tense – that is, marked and unmarked verb forms as well as a very specific SingE variant, which marks verbs for completion of an action by means of *finish* as a postverbal marker (VERB+finish).

---

[1] Note that the granularity of data analysis and the use of specific predictors may vary between the different substudies presented in this Element (e.g., *it* treated as one pronoun type or split up into different subtypes; the finer classification of LiBa introduced in Section 2.1.3). This is not necessarily due to linguistic motivations but is the result of experimenting with the data sets and predictors at the different stages of PrInDT development, and putting together initially individual substudies in this Element. This does, however, not pose a problem for the illustration of our approach; it rather highlights its flexibility.

[2] It has to be noted that the name "Test of Early Grammatical Impairment" is somewhat misleading here. The test had been developed to probe into potential language impairments in young children but has ever since also been employed for investigating "normally" developing children.

Table 2 Subject pronoun realization with unbalanced predictor: List of variables

Variable type	Variable	Levels	Abbreviation
Dependent	class	realized, zero	–
Independent	pronoun type	referential (refer) demonstrative (dem) expletive it (it_ex) referential it (it_ref) contextual referential it (it_con)	PRN_TYPE
Independent	mean length of utterance	2, 3, adult	MLU
Independent	(ethnic) group	Chinese children (C) Indian children (I) adults (ethnic group not available)	ETHN_GROUP
Independent	age	in months of the individual child for all adults = 216 months; numeric	AGE

1. Child: Then he **wanted** to climb a ladder to a chimney. Then the big bad wolf **is** in the pot. Then all the water **splash** and the carrot and the onion.
2. Child: He **eat finish** everything.

The forms in these examples are variably used by the Singaporean children and, again, are also typical of adult SingE and thus part of the input the children receive. The data include past-tense marking tokens by 29 male and female Singaporean children of different ethnicities, aged 2;5 to 12;1 (all bi- or multilingual) and 19 male and female children from England, aged 2;1 to 10;9 (bi-/multi- and monolingual). The aim of the analysis of these data is to find prediction rules for past-tense marking (*marked*, *unmarked*, and *finish*; i.e., the SingE variants) by means of extra- and intralinguistic predictors. The extralinguistic features considered as independent variables in the statistical analysis are, again, ethnicity (ETH), age (AGE), sex (SEX), linguistic background (LiBa), and mean length of utterance (MLU). The variables ETH, AGE, SEX, and MLU are defined as for the *subpro* data set in Section 2.1.1 (cf. Table 1). For LiBa, a finer distinction is used than in *subpro*. Here we distinguish the categories *bili1*, *bili2*, *mono*, *mono+*, *multi1*, and *multi2*, which are briefly explained as follows:

- Monolingual (*mono*): Children are exposed to and use only one language before primary school.
- Monolingual+ (*mono+*): Children who grow up monolingually and start learning a second language as late as the early school years.
- Bilingual1 (*bili1*): Children are exposed to and use two languages from before the age of two.
- Bilingual2 (*bili2*): Children are exposed to one language before the age of two and start acquiring/using the second language later than age two.
- Multilingual1 (*multi1*): Children are exposed to and use three or more languages from before the age of two.
- Multilingual2 (*multi2*): Children are exposed to and use two languages from before the age of two and start acquiring/using a third or fourth language later than age two.

For the past-tense study, we consider the variable VERB as an intralinguistic predictor. The levels of this variable are the nine most frequent verbs in the utterances of the children. For the remaining verbs, we consider the levels *reg* (regular) and *irreg* (irregular) only. As the nine most frequent verbs, we identified *be, blow, come, do, find, go, make, say,* and *want*, which mostly resulted from the specific elicitation tasks the children had completed. The PrInDT analyses of the data are presented in Sections 5.3 and 5.6; the underlying statistical methods are introduced in Sections 4.5.3 and 4.5.6.

2.1.4 Vowel Length

Based on the data set called *vowel*, we study the realization of long and short vowel contrasts in L1 child SingE, again compared to the data collected in England and by means of extra- and intralinguistic predictors. Since earlier studies have reported various vowel mergers for L2 SingE (e.g., Wee 2004: 1024–1026), which are often not based on substantial, quantifiable empirical evidence but on auditory impression only, Buschfeld (2020, chapter 8) measured quantity and quality contrasts between KIT and FLEECE and FOOT and GOOSE in her L1 child SingE data in Praat (Boersma & Weenink 2018). She could not attest a clear vowel-length merger since phone duration was phonemic for all groups of children, even if contrasts between both pairs were slightly weaker in the Singaporean children than in the children from England (Buschfeld 2020: 253).

Again, we take her analysis as a starting point. The data is thus part of the corpus collected by Buschfeld (2020) and was elicited by means of a self-developed picture naming task, which was geared toward triggering vowels in the lexical sets of KIT-FLEECE and FOOT-GOOSE (cf. Wells 1982) in a playful way. The picture-naming task contained six pictures for each set, aiming to elicit [ɪ] and [iː] and [ʊ] and [uː] vowel tokens (cf. Buschfeld 2020). For our PrInDT application, we focus on vowel-length realizations in the KIT-FLEECE productions of 22 male and female Singaporean children of different ethnicities, aged 2;6 to 12;1 (all multilingual) and 21 male and female children from England, aged 2;1 to 10;9 (multi- and monolingual). The exact vowel length of all KIT and FLEECE tokens was measured in Praat (Boersma & Weenink 2018). A total of 497 tokens, 225 of which were FLEECE tokens and 272 of which were KIT tokens, are available for analysis. Due to the elicitation experiment, tokens are distributed on a limited set of lexemes (cf. Table 3; for details on the exact methods of elicitation and data processing, cf. Buschfeld 2020: 90–92, 117–120).

Again, we apply different, more advanced statistical methods. In our main application of regression ctrees, the dependent variable is vowel length (in milliseconds, ms) of long- and short-vowel contrasts of KIT versus FLEECE sounds, which we model by means of extra- and intralinguistic predictors. As extralinguistic predictors we consider SEX, ETH, AGE, LiBa, and MLU, as defined in Table 1. Additionally, we consider the country with values E = England and S = Singapore. As intralinguistic predictors, we employ the variables in Table 3.

In Sections 3.2.1, 3.2.2, 3.2.3.1, 3.2.3.3, and 3.2.4, we analyze these data by means of classical statistical methods. Our PrInDT analyses of the data are presented in Sections 5.4 and 5.6. The underlying statistical methods are introduced in Sections 4.5.4 and 4.5.6.

2.2 Linguistic Landscaping on St. Martin

Another study we build on for introducing our full set of PrInDT approaches is the recent investigation of linguistic landscapes on the Eastern Caribbean island of St. Martin (Buschfeld, Weihs, & Ronan 2024). What makes the island exceptional for such an analysis is its small size but high degree of multilingualism. Factors such as strong migration flows and tourism have promoted this development, which, at their core, go back to times of European colonization and the division of the island into a French- and a Dutch-ruled part (for further details on its historical and linguistic development, see Buschfeld, Weihs, & Ronan 2024).

The data for this part of our PrInDT application were collected in Marigot, the capital of the northern, French side of St. Martin, and Philipsburg, the capital of the southern, Dutch part, in February 2020. On the one hand, we report and discuss the results of the study by Buschfeld, Weihs, and Ronan (2024) with slight modifications only (cf. Section 5.5) to complete the picture of how the underlying idea of PrInDT can be applied to various linguistic contexts and objectives. On the

Table 3 Intralinguistic predictors for vowel length

Variable	Levels	Abbreviation
phone label	KIT, FLEECE	phone_label
lexeme	for the FLEECE sound: bee, cheese, key, leaf, sea, cheek; for the KIT sound: ship, chicken, fish, scissors, pig, lips, print, stick	lexeme
number of syllables	1, 2	syllables
word duration	ms	word_duration
speech rate	word_duration/syllables	speed
vowel minimum pitch	hertz	vowel_minimum_pitch
vowel maximum pitch	hertz	vowel_maximum_pitch
vowel intensity mean	db	vowel_intensity_mean
formant F1 at 50% of vowel length	hertz	f1_fifty
formant F2 at 50% of vowel length	hertz	f2_fifty
duration of phone left of the vowel	ms	phone_left_1_duration
duration of phone right of the vowel	ms	phone_right_1_duration
class of consonant left of the vowel	l, r, tʃ, voiced plosive (vd. p), voiceless fricative (vl.f), voiceless plosive (vl.p)	cons_class_l
class of consonant right of the vowel	? (glottal stop), empty, nas (nasal), vd.f (voiced fricative), vd. p, vl.f, vl.p	cons_class_r

other hand, we apply further PrInDT methods to the data set (cf. Section 5.6). The main aim is to unveil potential differences between the linguistic landscapes of the formerly French- and Dutch-colonized parts of the island. The data were collected in the commercial districts of the two cities. In both cities, pictures were taken of shop windows, street and road signs, memorials, graffiti, and any type of sign that would fall within one of the categories traditionally employed for the classification of signs – that is, infrastructural, regulatory, commemorative, commercial, and unauthorized (cf. Ziegler et al. 2018).

The data set consists of 373 signs from Marigot and 372 signs from Philipsburg, and is thus fairly balanced in terms of the number of signs from each of the two locations. We analyzed each individual sign (i.e., "any piece of written text within a spatially definable frame"; Backhaus 2006: 55), in terms of languages it displays, regardless of the extent of the linguistic sample (i.e., from one-word units to longer stretches of text). The individual signs were then coded according to the characteristics presented in Table 4. Additionally, the researcher (two levels) who collected the data as well as the coder (three levels) were included as possible predictors for our three target variables (i.e., the presence of French, Dutch, and English as the three official and most frequently used languages in the respective parts of the island).

Admittedly, the coding scheme is complex, but we cannot go into all details here (as is also true for the previously introduced data sets), due to spatial restrictions and a focus on the statistical applications to be discussed in subsequent sections of this Element (cf. Buschfeld, Weihs, & Ronan 2024 for further details on the landscaping study). The corresponding data set is called *land*. For PrInDT analyses of the data, see Sections 5.5 and 5.6. The underlying statistical methods are introduced in Sections 4.5.5 and 4.5.6.

3 Setting the Statistical Background

Before we turn toward introducing the PrInDT approach and its different subversions and presenting our sample analyses of the different data sets in Sections 4 and 5, we briefly introduce R and the statistical approaches and principles on which PrInDT and its various subversions are based, with reference to the data sets introduced in Section 2.

3.1 Steps before Using PrInDT in R: Input, Presentation, and Transformation of Data

Before using the PrInDT package in R, it has to be installed and attached. Installation is necessary only once; attachment via the library function, however, is necessary in each new R session. In the following, we present the relevant R-code, which is accompanied by explanations wherever necessary, indicated by a hashtag (#).

```
install.packages('PrInDT') # installation of PrInDT package
library(PrInDT) # attach package
```

Table 4 Characteristics of signs

Variable	Levels	Abbreviation
location	Philipsburg, Marigot	location
type of sign	commercial (com), infrastructural (infra), regulatory (reg), commemorative (commem), unauthorized (trans)	type.of.sign
sign (narrow categorization of type of sign)	digital sign (digi), street sign (str), road sign (road), graffiti (graf), stand-up-display (stand), wall sign (wall), hanging sign (hang), sun-blind (sblind), sticker (stick; including posters), shop window (shopw), door sign (door)	sign
permanence	yes, no	permanent
proper noun included	brand name (bn), brand name+ (bn+), location (lo), location+ (lo+), restaurant name (rn), restaurant name+ (rn+), company name (cn), company name+ (cn+), no	proper.noun
number of languages	1, 2, 3, 4+	no.languages
language indicators	French, Dutch, English, Spanish, Italian, German (coded as 0 = no, 1 = yes)	French, Dutch, ...
brand name unclear	0 = no, 1 = yes if we could not specify the language of a brand name	bn.unclear
multilingual type	0 = monolingual signs 1 = fully complementary: duplicates the exact same information in all languages 2 = provides full information in one language and only select information in the other language(s) 3 = multilingual writing may have some information in one language and other information in one or more other languages; overlapping multilingual writing 4 = different parts of the signage are in different languages; complementary multilingual writing; no overlap or shared information	multilingual.type

In a next step, the basic data have to be read in. Depending on the format of the underlying data set, this needs to be done in different ways. The data have to be assigned to a so-called data frame with a specified name; here we simply use data. The assignment operator is <-, as illustrated in the following examples.

```
data <- load("dataset_name.RData") # data stored as an R data frame
data <- read.csv("dataset_name.csv") # data in a text file, comma separated
library(xlsx) # attach library with function read.xlsx2
data <- read.xlsx2("dataset_name.xlsx",1) # data in the first sheet of an Excel file
```

The PrInDT package contains random parts of the data sets introduced in Section 2, but not the full sets collected for the studies. Therefore, the R-code provided in Sections 3.2, 4, and 5 will not produce the reported results but only similar ones if applied to the data available in the package. The data in the PrInDT package can be loaded through the following codes:

```
data <- PrInDT::data_zero # subpro data set
data <- PrInDT::data_speaker # nessubpro data set
data <- PrInDT::data_past # past data set
data <- PrInDT::data_vowel # vowel data set
data <- PrInDT::data_land # land data set
```

The data frame data consists of a matrix in which each row corresponds to an observation and each column to a variable. Therefore, the number of rows (first dimension) is equal to the number of observations, and the number of columns (second dimension) is equal to the number of variables. To check the content of data, different presentation methods may be applied, for example:

```
str(data) # structure of data: variable names and values
View(data) # spreadsheet presentation
data$variable_name # list of all values of the variable variable_name
```

The $ sign separates the names of the data frame (data) and the respective variable (variable_name) in the data frame.

The functions of PrInDT are not programmed to automatically carry out any data transformations. If transformations of observed variables are employed as predictors in a PrInDT analysis, these must be carried out before the function call. In the *vowel* data set (cf. Section 2.1.4), for example, we need to define speed (per syllable) as the ratio of word duration and number of syllables, as done in the following call:

```
data$speed <- data$word_duration / data$syllables # division of two variables
```

3.2 Statistical Methods

We now turn toward those statistical methods that our different PrInDT approaches are based on.

3.2.1 Descriptive Statistics

Descriptive statistics provides characteristics of the data, such as mean or median, tables, and graphs, for summarizing and illustrating distributions of observations of variables and their relationships. A multitude of methods exist in descriptive statistics. For univariate descriptive methods, the interested reader is referred to, for example, Levshina (2015: 41, 69) and for bivariate methods to Levshina (2015: 115).

3.2.2 Inferential Statistics

Inferential statistics provides tests for statistically validating hypotheses on distributions and on relationships between variables in a specific population. The main idea in statistical testing is that we consider a variable for which the distribution is assumed to be known except for some unknown property. For example, for the variable vowel_length in Section 2.1.4 a normal distribution might be assumed with an unknown mean. In such a situation, in statistics, a so-called hypothesis about the unknown mean is stated: "The mean μ is equal to a certain value μ_0." This hypothesis is then tested by assessing the distance between μ_0 and the sample mean. The larger this distance, the less probable μ_0 is. One of the most well-known statistical tests is the so-called (one-sample) t-test. In a t-test, the so-called t-statistic is calculated by

$t = (\bar{x} - \mu_0)/\text{sd}(\bar{x})$ with $\text{sd}(\bar{x})$ = standard deviation of the mean.

The probability of the calculated value of the t-statistic and of even more extreme values is called the "p-value." If the p-value is very small (typically smaller than 0.05), we reject the hypothesis since the sample mean appears to be too improbable if the hypothesis is true.

As an example, we consider the hypothesis that the population mean (called "true mean" in R) of vowel_length is equal to $\mu_0 = 190$:

```
t.test(data$vowel_length,mu=190)
```

One Sample t-test
data: data$vowel_length
t = 2.2196, df = 496, p-value = 0.0269
alternative hypothesis: true mean is not equal to 190

95 percent confidence interval:
191.0651 207.4907
sample estimates:
mean of x
199.2779

Since the p-value is 0.027, the hypothesis is rejected. For vowel_length, the sample mean is 199.2779 and its so-called 95% confidence interval is [191.0651, 207.4907] (cf. the R-output). This confidence interval covers the true mean with 95% probability if the hypothesis is true. The hypothesized value 190 does not lie in this interval, which again supports that $\mu_0 = 190$ is rejected as potential population mean.

Such t-tests are also applied for testing the significance of an estimate of an unknown coefficient in, for example, a linear model (cf. Section 3.2.3.1). For conditional inference trees, we apply so-called two-sample tests that compare the distribution of a variable for different populations. This is discussed in Section 3.2.3.3.

3.2.3 Statistical Models: Regression and Classification

Statistical models represent the relationship between variables and combine both descriptive and inferential statistics. On the one hand, a statistical model attempts to represent the relationship between a so-called dependent variable (target) and one or more so-called independent variables (predictors) by means of a descriptive mathematical formula, for example, motivated by earlier theoretical assumptions or a prior analysis. On the other hand, it is an important goal of statistical modeling to test the so-called significance of the influence of potential predictors on the dependent variable. We distinguish two types of models: classification and regression models. For classification models, the dependent variable is categorical (i.e., represents categories, so-called classes); for regression models, the dependent variable is a continuous quantity.

Statistical models typically used in linguistic analyses include various kinds of linear regression models (fixed effects, mixed effects; cf. Section 3.2.3.1) and specific nonlinear models like logistic models in classification (i.e., for categorical dependent variables; cf. Section 3.2.3.2). These types of models rely on the idea of optimizing a fit criterion, namely minimizing the least squares error (for linear models) – that is, the sum of squared differences between observations and model values – or maximizing the probability that the model is true (for logistic models). For the following discussion of classification and regression modeling (Sections 3.2.3.1 and 3.2.3.2), we employ two of the data sets introduced in Section 2, namely the *subpro* data set for classification and the *vowel* data set for regression.

3.2.3.1 Linear Models

For linear modeling, we assume a linear relationship between a continuous target variable Y and K predictor variables $X_j, j = 1, \ldots, K$. The idea is to look for the best model of the type

$$y_i = \beta_0 + \beta_1 * x_{i1} + \ldots + \beta_K * x_{iK} + \varepsilon_i,$$

where $i = 1, \ldots, n$ is the observation number; $\beta_0, \beta_1, \ldots, \beta_K$ are unknown model coefficients; and ε is a (normally distributed) model error. β_0 is the model constant, called "intercept"; the other βs are the multipliers of the predictors, called "slopes."

As an example, consider the data set *vowel* (cf. Section 2.1.4), in which vowel_length is the target variable and vowel_maximum_pitch and vowel_minimum_pitch are the predictor variables:

$$\text{vowel\_length}_i = \beta_0 + \beta_1 * \text{vowel\_maximum\_pitch}_i + \beta_2 * \text{vowel\_minimum\_pitch}_i + \varepsilon_i.$$

In this model, the number of tokens (n) amounts to 497, and the number of predictors (K) is 2. To identify the best values for $\beta_0, \beta_1, \ldots, \beta_K$, the so-called least squares criterion is applied (i.e., we minimize the following squared distance between the target and the model):

$$\sum_{i=1}^{n} (y_i - \beta_0 - \beta_1 * x_{i1} - \ldots - \beta_K * x_{iK})^2.$$

The values minimizing this criterion are the so-called least squares estimates. In R, linear modeling (lm) is applied by means of the following code:

```
mvow <- lm(vowel_length ~ vowel_maximum_pitch +
                    vowel_minimum_pitch,data=data)
summary(mvow) # model output including the following lines
```

	Estimate	Std. Error	t value	Pr(>|t|)	
(Intercept)	187.72465	15.38522	12.202	<2e–16	***
vowel_maximum_pitch	0.45828	0.04747	9.654	<2e–16	***
vowel_minimum_pitch	-0.57093	0.05992	-9.528	<2e–16	***

The output of lm is assigned to the list mvow. The estimated coefficients (Estimate) and some indicators of their uncertainty (Standard Error, t-value, Pr(>|t|)) are part of the output of the summary statement. The column "Pr(>|t|)" gives the p-value of the t-test on the hypothesis "true value of the coefficient = 0."

This hypothesis should be rejected since otherwise the corresponding variable would probably not have any influence on the target, in our example on vowel length. Significance of rejection is typically defined by means of a threshold for the p-value. Such thresholds can be set differently. In our example, the threshold is set to 5%, which is often the case in linguistic modeling. This is indicated by "*" in the last column, "**" indicates that the p-value is smaller than 1%, and "***" indicates that the p-value is smaller than 0.1%.

In our model, all predictors are highly significant (i.e., their slopes are unequal to zero at the 0.1% level). Thus we can argue that the predictors have a significant influence on the target. The model can be interpreted as follows: vowel_length significantly depends linearly on both vowel_maximum_pitch and vowel_minimum_pitch. If vowel_maximum_pitch is increased by 10 Hz, then vowel_length, on average, increases by 4.6 ms (estimate for vowel_maximum_pitch = 0.458). If vowel_minimum_pitch is increased by 10 Hz, then vowel_length decreases by 5.7 ms (estimate = –0.571).

Unfortunately, this procedure is only well-defined for continuous predictors X_k. For categorical predictors, for each value except one, the so-called reference value, an additional constant is estimated, which is added to the constant of the reference value. Such a constant can be interpreted as a correction of the intercept corresponding to a value of the categorical variable, which is not the reference value. In R, the reference value can be set by the user. If set automatically, the alphabetically first value is selected.

As an example, we consider the influence of two categorical variables, country (with two values *E* for England [= reference] and *S* for Singapore) and phone_label (with two values *fleece* [= reference] and *kit*) on vowel_length. Does vowel_length depend on country and phone_label? Are different increments necessary for the different values of these two variables?

Sometimes a corrective constant depends on the values of other variables. In such cases, we talk about so-called interactions between variables. For example, for two categorical variables the estimate of the interaction of two specific values of the two variables corrects the estimated constants of the two values. This will also be illustrated by the example of vowel length influenced by the two variables country and phone_label. In R, interactions are coded by the notation $X_1:X_2$. The model term X_1*X_2 is a short notation for including the intercept, the individual effects of X_1 and X_2, and the interaction $X_1:X_2$ in the model. We employed the following R-code:

```
mcvowi <- lm(vowel_length ~ country*phone_label,data=data)
summary(mcvowi)
```

	Estimate	Std. Error	t value	Pr(>|t|)	
(Intercept)	266.916	8.048	33.164	<2e−16	***
countryS	−34.238	10.885	−3.145	0.00176	**
phone_labelkit	−109.734	10.734	−10.223	<2e−16	***
countryS:phone_labelkit	37.379	14.690	2.545	0.01125	*

This model can be interpreted as follows: vowel_length depends on both country (England versus Singapore) and phone label (*fleece* versus *kit*) in the following way: For Singaporean children (countryS), vowel_length is shorter than for children growing up in England (reference level) by (on average) 34 ms. For the label *kit* (phone_labelkit), vowel length is shorter by (on average) 110 ms than for the label *fleece* (reference level). However, the combination of country=Singapore and phone_label=*kit* (countryS:phone_labelkit) has an additional effect on vowel length of (on average) 37 ms. The overall effect of a specific combination of levels of the two predictors depends on the realized levels. For example, the combination (country=Singapore, phone_label=*kit*) has an overall effect on vowel length of the sum of all estimates (i.e., of [rounded] 267 − 34 − 110 + 37 = 160 ms), whereas, for example, the overall effect of the combination (country=England, phone_label=*fleece*) is represented by the intercept of 267 ms.

In a next step, we combine the two models mvow and mcvowi, as introduced earlier in this section, to a model that jointly represents dependencies on both continuous and categorical predictors:

```
mcvowa <- lm(vowel_length ~ country*phone_label + vowel_maximum_pitch +
        vowel_minimum_pitch,data=data)
summary(mcvowa)
```

	Estimate	Std.Error	t value	Pr(>|t|)	
(Intercept)	238.44426	15.12258	15.767	<2e−16	***
countryS	−32.32962	10.00153	−3.232	0.00131	**
phone_labelkit	−94.25573	10.03167	−9.396	<2e−16	***
vowel_maximum_pitch	0.37987	0.04306	8.821	<2e−16	***
vowel_minimum_pitch	−0.43172	0.05506	−7.841	2.8e−14	***
countryS:phone_labelkit	35.86929	13.51012	2.655	0.00819	**

As we can see, the estimated slopes are similar but not identical to the corresponding slopes in the models mvow and mcvowi. In particular, the effect sizes of the pitch variables considerably change by including country and phone_label in the model. Still, all effects are highly significant.

The effect of a variable that represents a random choice from a larger population, like the children in the *vowel* data set, is typically modeled by a so-called stochastic term (i.e., as a so-called random effect), resulting in a so-called mixed-effects linear model. In contrast, for predictors for which we only want to study values with limited and concrete representations, we look for so-called fixed effects. One example is the predictor country, for which we want the model to be valid only for England and Singapore. Mixed-effects linear models will be discussed further in Section 3.2.4.

3.2.3.2 Logistic Models

For classification problems, we will focus on binary target variables Y – that is, target variables with two categories, coded by the values 0 and 1. Still, logistic regression can also be applied if a target has more than two values (cf., e.g., Levshina 2015: 277). In so-called logistic regression, we do not model this target variable directly but the probability π_1 of 1. To guarantee that this value lies between 0 and 1 (as a probability should), we use the model

$$\pi_1 = 1/(1+\exp(-(\beta_0+\beta_1*x_1+\ldots+\beta_K*x_K))).$$

This so-called logistic model only takes values between 0 and 1. This is illustrated in Figure 1, which is generated by the following R-code:

```
curve(1/(1+exp(-x)),from=-6,to=6)
```

The estimation of the unknown parameters β_0, β_1, ..., β_K is called "logistic regression." The corresponding R function is glm (generalized linear model) with the option family = binomial (with a binomial distribution being the sum of distributions with values 0 and 1 as for the classes in classification; for further

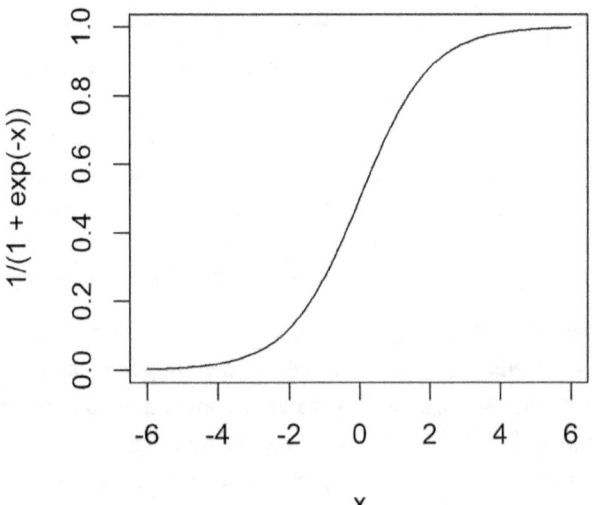

Figure 1 Logistic model.

details, see, e.g., Winter 2020: 198). Categorical predictors are treated in the same way as linear regression (cf. Section 3.2.3.1). After estimation of the parameters, the probability π_1 of 1 can be estimated for any values of the predictors. If it is larger than 0.5, class 1 is estimated; if not, class 0 is predicted.

In the following code, we illustrate logistic regression by means of the *subpro* data set. In the R-code, we use the model specification "real ~ .," which indicates that all variables in the data should be used as predictors except the target variable "real." In R, elements of data frames are typically referenced by the index pair [i,j], meaning the ith observation of the jth variable. The expression [,-1] stands for the elimination of variable 1, which is the variable CHILD in our data. The full R-code appears as follows:

```
CHILDzero <- datachild$CHILD # definition of the variable CHILDzero
data <- datachild[,-1] # elimination of CHILD from predictors
data <- na.omit(data) # elimination of missing values
logmod <- glm(real ~ .,data=data,family=binomial)
summary(logmod)
```

Table 5 Parameter estimates of logistic model

	Estimate	**Pr(>|z|)**	**Significance level**
(Intercept)	−2.217e+00	<2e−16	***
AGE	9.834e−05	0.980257	–
LiBamulti	−9.937e−01	0.267670	–
LiBaNA	−1.979e+00	0.088035	.
ETHE/m	5.573e−01	0.554553	–
ETHE/migr	6.108e−01	0.483164	–
ETHS/C	1.570e+00	0.081876	.
ETHS/I	1.217e+00	0.178987	–
ETHS/m	7.129e−01	0.479759	–
SEXmale	2.825e−01	0.037918	*
MLU2	−8.843e−01	1.09e−05	***
MLU3	−1.251e+00	0.000147	***
MLUOL	−2.557e−01	0.244523	–
PRNI	7.117e−02	0.632970	–
PRNit	1.799e+00	<2e−16	***
PRNshe	1.501e−01	0.441049	–
PRNthey	−8.266e−02	0.749988	–
PRNwe	−1.014e+00	0.005294	**
PRNyou_s	−9.800e−01	0.000771	***

The results of our glm application can be found in Table 5. We can see that at a 5% level, only SEXmale, MLU2, MLU3, PRNit, PRNwe, and PRNyou_s are significant. The only continuous predictor in the model is AGE, and its estimated coefficient is close to zero and thus not significant. Moreover, the model includes constants for the categories of the discrete predictors, which are nonsignificant but cannot be eliminated since other constants of this categorical variable are (partly highly) significant. For example, for PRN, the dummies PRNit, PRNwe, and PRNyou_s are highly significant, but the dummies for the other pronouns *I*, *she*, and *they* are insignificant. The levels *it*, *we*, and *you_s* will also turn up as important predictors in the corresponding PrInDT trees (cf. Figure 5, Section 5.1).

3.2.3.3 Decision Trees

Decision trees follow quite a different approach. They aim to characterize the data structure by means of binary partition of the data space via "splits" of the data based on individual predictors. In each split, an "if" condition is specified that splits the data into two subparts: one where the condition holds true and one where it does not. For example, if Singaporean children are of Chinese origin, they tend to leave out subject pronouns; if they are not, they do not. This generates two subparts of the data: one for Singaporean children of Chinese origin, and one for children of various other origins. In decision trees, such rules are selected as follows. In classification (cf. Section 3.2.3), splits are chosen so that the frequencies of realizations of the levels that represent the target variable differ as much as possible in the generated subparts. In regression, splits are chosen so that the distribution of the continuous target variable is as different as possible in the subparts. In the subparts, follow-up splits again look for the best partitions. This leads to a series of so-called if-then rules.

In the so-called terminal nodes of a tree (i.e., in the nodes that are not split anymore), a decision is made about the prediction of the dependent variable, for example, whether under the conditions leading to the respective node *zero* subject pronouns are used or whether pronouns are *realized*. In a terminal node, the distribution of all values of the target variable, which are assigned to the node following the if-then rules, is displayed. For continuous targets, this distribution is illustrated by a box-plot (for an introduction to box-plots, see, e.g., Levshina 2015: 57); for binary targets the frequencies of the two classes are presented in different gray shades. As the predicted value generated by the terminal node, only one representative value is taken from these distributions – namely the most frequent class in classification and in regression the mean of all values of the target variable.

Up to this point, we have introduced the generation of decision trees from a solely descriptive perspective (i.e., without considering statistical inference). This is taken into account by so-called conditional inference trees (ctrees; Hothorn et al. 2006), in which the splits are chosen on the basis of p-values, which are generated to test the underlying hypothesis that the distribution of the target is equal in the generated subparts. The more significantly this hypothesis is rejected (i.e., the smaller the p-value), the more relevant the split. Therefore, the split with the smallest p-value is realized in the tree. The maximum p-value accepted for a split (i.e., the maximum significance level of the tree) is typically specified as 5% or 1%.

In the following code, we generate a ctree for the same set of predictors for which we generated mcvowa in Section 3.2.3.1 – that is, for the predictors country, phone_label, vowel_maximum_pitch, and vowel_minimum_pitch as potentially influencing the target vowel_length. The corresponding R-code reads as follows:

```
library(party) # function ctree is in the package party
ctvowa <- ctree(vowel_length ~ country + phone_label + vowel_maximum_pitch +
    vowel_minimum_pitch,data=data)
plot(ctvowa)
```

The plot of the tree in Figure 2 shows the decision variables in the nodes together with the p-value of the test on the equality of the distributions in the two subnodes. Which part of the data occurs on the left and on the right is indicated by the value(s) of the relevant decision variable on the lines connecting the nodes. For example, the first split at the top of the tree (i.e., phone_label) sorts FLEECE vowels into the left subnode and KIT vowels into the right subnode. For continuous variables like vowel_maximum_pitch, splits are characterized by inequalities. For example, observations with vowel_maximum_pitch >319.5 Hz are part of the right split, while the rest of the values go into the left split (Node 2).

As an example for an if-then rule of the tree in Figure 2, we report the rule for Node 3. If phone_label=*fleece* and vowel_maximum_pitch $\leq$ 319.5 Hz, then vowel_length is predicted as the mean of the lengths of all vowels for which these two properties are true.

Another important property of a decision tree is that it automatically identifies interactions between predictors (cf. Section 3.2.3.1). For example, the complete left part of the tree is only valid if phone_label=*fleece* (i.e., the following splits depend on this first condition). The decisions in the left and the right part of the tree are typically different so that, in our example, the effects of vowel_maximum_pitch and vowel_minimum_pitch depend on the value of

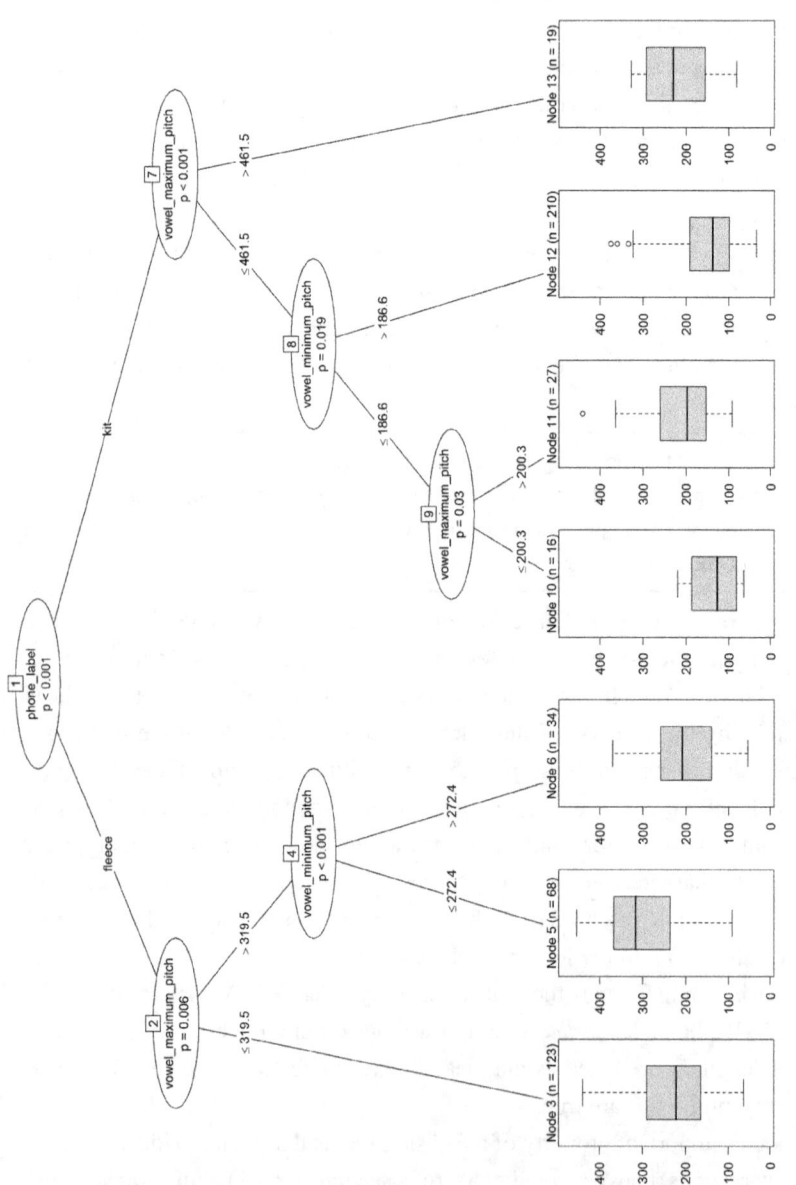

Figure 2 Tree for vowel length.

phone_label. Therefore, interactions are not explicitly but implicitly modeled in decision trees.

In a next step, we generate a decision tree for the classification problem for which we built a logistic regression model in Section 3.2.3.2 (i.e., for the realization of subject pronouns). The tree is based on the following R-code:

```
library(party)
# data - subpro data
ctsub <- ctree(real ~ .,data=data,control=ctree_control(mincriterion=0.99))
plot(ctsub)
```

The control parameter mincriterion states that the maximum significance level in the splits should be 1 – 0.99 = 0.01. The standard value for this parameter would be 0.95. This would generate a much larger and more complex tree, which is why we lowered the significance level for ease of illustration and interpretability.

In the terminal nodes of the tree in Figure 3, the shares of the two classes *zero* (in dark gray) and *realized* (in light gray) are displayed. In addition to those predictors, identified as significant by the logistic regression model (cf. Section 3.2.3.2), the tree includes splits in the variables ETH and LiBa, which were only significant at the 10% level for logistic regression, and even a split in AGE, which was insignificant for logistic regression. This finding shows that trees identify other kinds of significant relationships. This is also discussed by Gries (2020). He points out that trees might even be unable to find the correct predictors-response relationship. The discrepancies in the findings of linear models and trees, however, are not too surprising and not necessarily due to one approach being superior over the other. They are rather due to different approaches focusing on different statistical relations and thus may produce slightly different findings. Basic linear modeling, for example, assesses the significance of the influences of given predictors (main effects), whereas decision trees mainly identify (significant) interactions between these predictors. In the best case, these two kinds of models complement each other (cf. Tagliamonte & Baayen 2012 for a corresponding discussion). For us, decision trees have the advantage that their "if-then" rules are much easier and more straightforward to interpret than the linear combinations of linear models, in particular for novice users of statistical methods.

An often-used generalization of decision trees are random forests. They consist of many trees generated by resampling (i.e., by taking different random subsamples from the observed sample and estimating the tree based on these samples; cf. Section 3.2.6). This is a recognized and often used method to counteract overfitting (i.e., that the model fits the training data extremely well

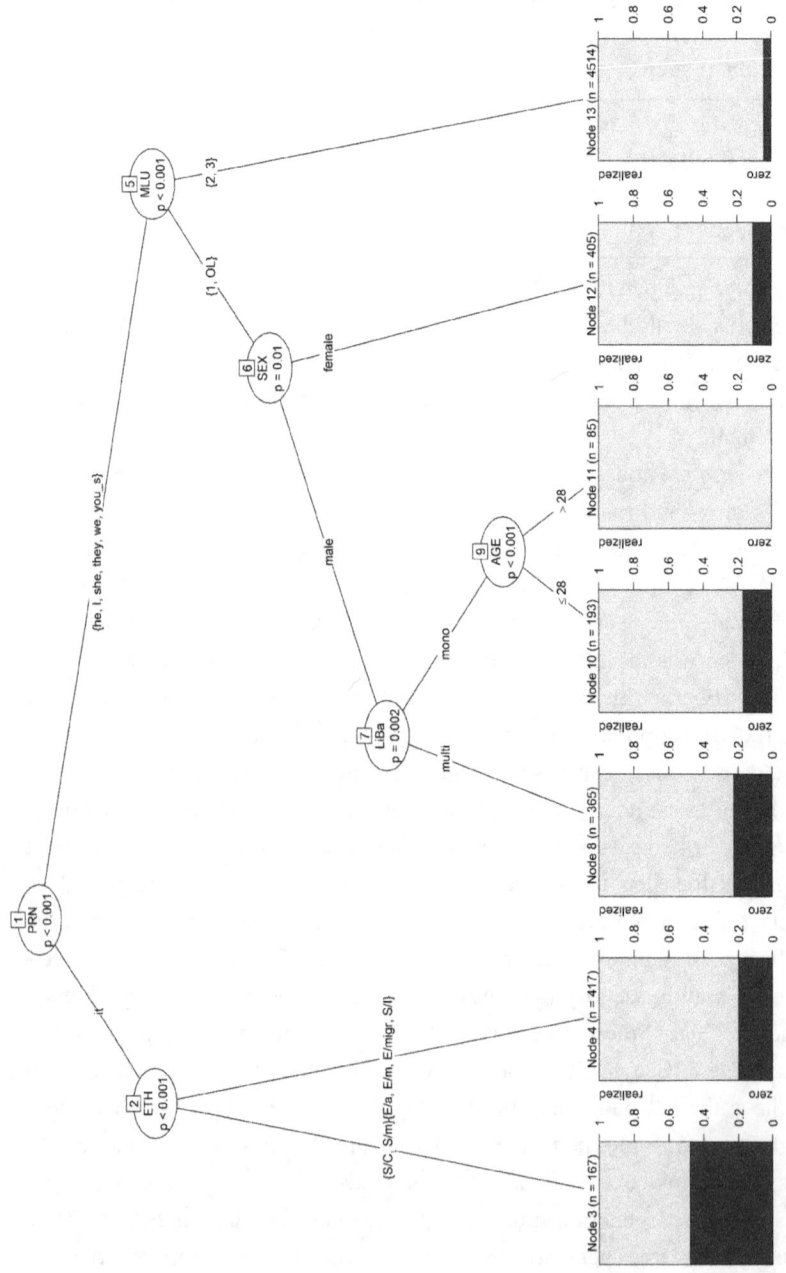

Figure 3 Tree for subject-pronoun realization.

but does not match the behavior of the overall population). By leaving out parts of the observed data for model construction, the validity of the models can be evaluated on these left-out parts of the data (test sample). In this Element, we utilize the idea of random forests to identify the best model. The optimization criterion we employ is "accuracy on the full sample," combining the accuracies on the training sample (fit) with the accuracy on the test sample, which represents the predictive power of the model. In our approach, we take into consideration Gries' (2020) criticism that a summary of the trees of a random forest might be inadequate. Such a summary might consist of the most representative tree according to a distance measure between the trees (cf. Laabs et al. 2024; i.e. the tree which is closest to all other trees). Instead, we evaluate the individual trees of a forest to identify the best tree (cf. Section 3.2.6) – that is, we do not employ a summary of all trees of a forest, but use the forest only as material to identify the best tree by evaluating an accuracy measure.

3.2.4 Model Accuracy

There is no question that the aspects discussed in the preceding sections are all relevant for model selection. However, it ultimately strongly depends on your research questions and hypotheses which models are best suited for the respective analysis, but often more than one approach is suitable for the envisaged investigation. It may thus be sensible to not simply choose the first available approach or simply the approach most "hip" in the discipline but to compare different models, not only in terms of their results but, in particular, also their accuracies. While linguists with strong statistical expertise, of course, consider such aspects and model accuracy in their approaches, model validation still comes up short in many linguistic investigations (cf. Buschfeld, Leuckert, et al. 2024). This is why our approach stresses the importance of evaluating model accuracy. In the following sections (Sections 3.2.4.1–3.2.4.2), we therefore introduce model accuracy for regression and classification models.

3.2.4.1 Regression Models

Linear and nonlinear regression models rely on the idea of optimizing a fit criterion, namely minimizing the least squares error (for linear models; i.e., the sum of squared differences between observations and model values) or maximizing the probability that the model is true (for logistic models). Therefore, such models are called "globally optimal" since they optimize criteria like the goodness of fit on the full data set. Accordingly, linear and nonlinear regression models come up with measures for the overall accuracy of the model that are related to the construction of the models. One of the most prominent measures is the

$$\text{goodness of fit} = R^2 = (\text{variance of } y \text{ explained by the model})/(\text{total variance of } y).$$

The more total variance of the target explained by the model (i.e., the closer R^2 is to 1), the better the model fit.

In the following code, we compare the R^2 of the models we looked at in Section 3.2.3.1. For the model mvow, we get an $R^2 = 0.20$, and for the model mcvowa, we get an $R^2 = 0.36$. Therefore, the additional categorical predictors added to mcvowa increase the goodness of fit by 0.16. The R^2s are automatically included in the output created by the following summary statement:

```
mcvowa <- lm(vowel_length ~ country*phone_label + vowel_maximum_pitch +
        vowel_minimum_pitch,data=data)
summary(mcvowa)
```

Aside from the estimations shown in Section 3.2.3.1, the summary statement creates the information "Multiple R-squared: 0.3645."

Let us finally compare the R^2 of the regression tree ctvowa presented in Section 3.2.3.3 with the R^2 for the regression model mcvowa. R^2s of decision trees have to be calculated explicitly, which can be done by means of the following statement:

```
pred <- predict(ctvowa) # predict function for ctrees
R2 <- 1 - sum((pred - data$vowel_length)^2) / sum((data$vowel_length -
    mean(data$vowel_length))^2)
```

This leads to an $R^2 = 0.35$, which is similar to the $R^2 = 0.36$ for the corresponding linear regression model mcvowa.

Overall, the model fit of all these regression models is not satisfactory since the R^2s are so low. However, we could use the other possible predictors in the *vowel* data set to improve model quality. Unfortunately, if we use all available predictors, predictors with partial overlaps in their levels (e.g., MLU and AGE, both relating to the children's linguistic development) influence each other in ways that make model estimation and interpretation difficult. Therefore, we decided to eliminate such correlated features (for a definition of a correlation matrix, cf. Levshina 2015: 134). To identify the highest correlations, we first transformed all factor levels into numerical values to be able to use "standard correlation" and then calculated the correlation matrix by means of the following R-code:

```
datan <- as.data.frame(sapply(data,as.numeric)) # transformation to numeric
cor(datan) > 0.88 # highest correlations
```

This identifies the correlations between MLU and AGE and between ETH and country as highest. Therefore, we decided to leave out MLU and ETH from further analyses.

On this data set, we applied the mixed-effects models introduced in Section 3.2.3.1. We start with a model including the stochastic factor lexeme. To apply a stepwise function to identify the significant influences, we utilized the library lmerTest and the following R-code:

```
library(lmerTest)
data$cons_class_r <- relevel(data$cons_class_r,"empty") # "empty" as reference level
lmerTestvow <- lmer(vowel_length ~ LiBa+phone_label+phone_left_1_duration+
    phone_right_1_duration+word_duration+vowel_minimum_pitch+
    vowel_maximum_pitch+vowel_intensity_mean+f1_fifty+f2_fifty+
    cons_class_l+cons_class_r+country+SEX+AGE+syllables+speed+(1|lexeme),
    data=data)
lmerstep <- step(lmerTestvow)
# stepwise identification of significant influences at 5% level
finalvow <- get_model(lmerstep) # transformation into a model summary(finalvow)
library(MuMIn) # library with the function r.squaredGLMM
r.squaredGLMM(finalvow)
```

The parameter estimates can be found in Table 6. For this model, we have to install the package MuMin to generate the so-called marginal R^2_m for the model with fixed effects only and R^2_c, the so-called conditional R^2, for both the fixed and the random effects together. This produces the goodness of fit measures $R^2_m = 0.4110$ and $R^2_c = 0.6068$.

Specifying a stochastic effect for the intercept by (1|lexeme) generates estimates of individual intercepts for each observed value of, in our case, lexeme. These estimates can be illustrated by means of coef(finalvow)$lexeme and can be used as intercepts for values of the lexeme used in the training set of the model. For new levels of the random effects, no such coefficient is available and only the fixed-effects part of the model can be used for prediction. On this basis, the relevant R^2 for the goodness of prediction (cf. Section 3.2.6) is $R^2_m = 0.41$, which is not much higher than the $R^2_m = 0.36$ of mcvowa.

In what follows, we will compare the estimated model from linear mixed-effects regression with a regression tree estimated on the full sample concerning model structure and accuracy. In the estimation of this tree, we include lexeme

Table 6 Parameter estimates of mixed-effects linear model with (1|lexeme)

Random effect	Std.dev.	–	–
lexeme	43.47	–	–
Fixed effects	estimate	Pr(>|t|)	signif.
intercept	200.91524	1.58e−08	***
word_duration	0.11324	<2e−16	***
vowel_min.pitch	−0.25769	1.04e−07	***
vowel_max_pitch	0.29799	3.07e−15	***
cons_class_r?	−45.54677	0.2252	–
cons_class_rnas	−21.97846	0.4527	–
cons_class_rvd.f	7.62385	0.7084	–
cons_class_rvd.p	−75.12605	0.0402	*
cons_class_rvl.f	7.86326	0.7845	–
cons_class_rvl.p	−70.43859	0.0160	*
countryS	−29.38133	1.06e−06	***
syllables	−80.05397	1.24e−07	***

as a fixed-effect factor and exclude CHILD, which we assume to be stochastic (for a more detailed discussion of stochastic factors in decision trees, cf. Section 4.5.1).

```
CHILDvowel <- data$Nickname
data$Nickname <- NULL # elimination of CHILD from dataset
finaltreevow <- ctree(vowel_length ~ .,data=data)
```

This leads to an R^2 of 0.4745, which is higher than $R^2_m = 0.4110$ but lower than $R^2_c = 0.6068$ for the corresponding linear mixed-effects model finalvow, presented previously. As Figure 4 illustrates, lexeme initiates only the first (root) split in the tree model, separating long vowels (at the left) from shorter ones. Only "Cheek" appears to be misplaced when following standard pronunciation. Such splits are admittedly less detailed than estimating individual increments, as in the linear model. However, as can be seen, the tree identifies a (natural) grouping of the lexemes. Overall, the linear mixed-effects model and decision tree have quite a different structure and thus give very different insights, which might be interesting to compare and combine. The first model only estimates main effects, whereas the second model mainly estimates interactions. For example, cons_class_r and vowel_minimum_pitch only play a role if lexeme is not {Bee, Cheese, Key, Leaf, Sea}. For a comparison of these models with our optimized regression trees, see Section 5.4.2.

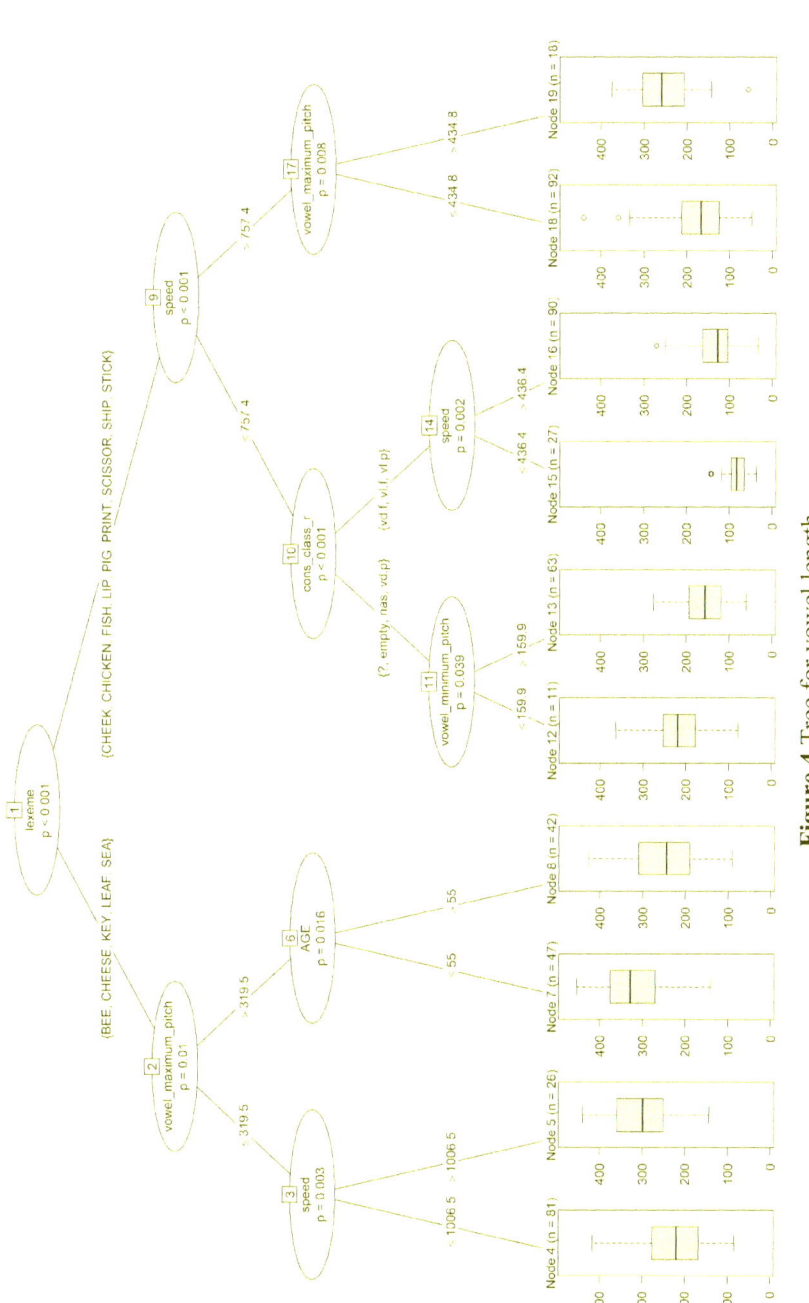

Figure 4 Tree for vowel length.

For the sake of completeness, we would like to mention that if we included the stochastic term (1|CHILD) in the estimation of the linear mixed-effects model, the goodness of fit measures would be $R^2_m = 0.4047$ and $R^2_c = 0.6542$ and the estimates of the fixed effects would be similar, but not identical, to the model without (1|CHILD).

In general, a plot like the one illustrated in Figure 4 is easy to interpret and normally suffices for a straightforward interpretation of decision trees. We ignore the bad fit here, as the focus is simply on the interpretability of the graph. The effects of the predictors of a (mixed-effects) linear model and their dependencies can be visualized by means of various plotting aids in R – for example, by means of the package sjPlot for *Data Visualization for Statistics in Social Science* (Lüdecke 2024).

For logistic regression models, too, a mixed-effects variant exists (cf., e.g., Winter 2020: 267). Furthermore, scholars have worked with Bayesian generalizations of the function lmer. For reasons of restrictions in space, we will not further discuss the Bayesian approach here, in particular since it is not relevant for the presentation and discussion of our approach (but see, e.g., Levshina 2022 for a comparison of Bayesian and frequentist models, and Winter & Bürkner 2021 for an application of Bayesian mixed-effects models).

3.2.4.2 Classification Models

For classification models, various methods exist for measuring accuracy. In linguistic studies, overall accuracy is often used since it is a straightforward and easy-to-apply method, even for statistical novices. The underlying formula is simple and overall accuracy thus easy to calculate:

overall accuracy = (number of correct predictions) / (total number of observations).

We will illustrate this with reference to the logistic regression model logmod (cf. Section 3.2.3.2), for which class coding is carried out alphabetically: 0 = *realized*, 1 = *zero*. To calculate the overall accuracy, a comparison of predictions and observed values of the target is needed. We consider the so-called confusion matrix for a detailed comparison of the observed classes and their predictions. In this matrix, each column sum equals the number of actual observations in the class indicated at the top (e.g., 5618 = 5600 + 18 observations for *realized* in the confusion matrix provided as follows). Each row presents the numbers of predictions of the class indicated in the left column for each class indicated in the top row. For example, the class *zero* is correctly predicted in 19 cases, but also incorrectly in 18 cases instead of the class *realized*.

```
pred <- predict(logmod,type="response") # predict probabilities of 1="zero"
prediction <- rep(0, dim(data)[1]) # default: prediction = 0 for all observations
prediction[pred > .5] <- 1 # correction to prediction = 1 = "zero", if probability > 0.5
table(prediction,data$real)
```

```
prediction    realized    zero
0             5600        509     # 0 stands for "realized"
1             18          19
```

Therefore, the overall accuracy is 0.914 (= (5600 + 19) / (5618 + 528)). At first glance, this is a very good result. However, it is misleading since while the large class *realized* is nearly always correctly predicted, the smaller class *zero* is underpredicted (i.e. in only 19 of 528 cases is *zero* correctly predicted; cf. our discussion of this common linguistic problem in Section 1). Therefore, this model is inadequate for prediction.

Unfortunately, for unbalanced classification problems, decision trees often neglect the smaller class, too. This, again, is demonstrated by means of a confusion matrix for the tree ctsub, which corresponds to the logistic regression model logmod:

```
prediction <- predict(ctsub)
table(prediction,data$real)
```

```
prediction    realized    zero
realized      5618        528
zero          0           0
```

Since for the tree ctsub the smaller class *zero* is never predicted, this model is inadequate for prediction, too. As stated in the introduction to this Element (Section 1), this problem was one of the main reasons and motivations for the development of the PrInDT approach (cf. Section 4.1 for further discussion).

3.2.5 Model Interpretation

Another important aspect of statistical modeling is the interpretability of the resulting model. Sometimes statistical models may predict results that go against all earlier linguistic assumptions and theoretical approaches. This may imply two things: Either the model is accidentally wrong in whatever it predicts or earlier theoretical assumptions are. When starting the collaboration, we encountered such a case in the modeling of the Singapore data and thus decided to make interpretability a major aspect of our approach. As further elaborated on in Section 4.2, this procedure is also an interesting means of validating earlier theoretical assumptions, and our observations suggest that restricting trees in their possible combinations of values might be a valid option to avoid an accidental misinterpretation of data and results. A tree chosen for analysis must be fully interpretable in order for us to compare the model to earlier results from similar research questions or put to the test existing theoretical approaches (for details, cf. Section 4.2). In general, we would claim that interpretability is a prerequisite for the assessment of model validity (cf. Gries 2020 for a discussion).

Unfortunately, interpretation is only easy and straightforward for comparatively small trees, since the interaction of many "if-then rules" makes trees rather difficult to process and understand. The size of the tree can easily be controlled for ctrees, since we can manually set the significance level, which indirectly determines the size of the tree. (The lower the significance level, the smaller the tree; cf. Section 3.2.3.3.) This is also true for linear models: The lower the maximally accepted significance level, the smaller the model.

Still, the question remains of which tree should be interpreted. Should one use the tree based on all observations? Or do "better" trees exist? We suggest that only models which are fully interpretable and come with high accuracy should be interpreted. High accuracy, however, is relative, and different scientific disciplines would set different standards here. This question has not yet been conclusively discussed by linguists. Winter (2020) and Sonderegger (2023) turn toward this problem for regression models and suggest that an accuracy of 0.7 would be unusually high for a linguistic study (Winter 2020: 77) and that stochastic effects often account for major parts of rather high accuracies (Sonderegger 2023: 278–279). In the social sciences, 0.5 seems to be treated as an acceptable level (Fernando 2024). We would agree that every model with an accuracy below 50% should be scrutinized. For classification models, experience has shown that accuracy rates of 70% and higher can be treated as very reliable and strong. The generation of models with high accuracy is at the core of our approach, which is why we will discuss strategies for optimizing the accuracy of ctrees in Section 4.3. Please note that we use the term *accuracy* in a broader sense than usual, since we aim for the optimization of a combination of goodness of fit and predictive power (cf. next section).

3.2.6 Real Prediction with Statistical Models: Resampling

Another shortcoming of many linguistic studies that make use of inferential statistical methods is that they do not consider real prediction (i.e., the transferability of the results beyond the observed sample to a wider population; cf. Buschfeld, Leuckert, et al. 2024). For the prediction of observations of the target variable that were used for model construction, we hope for a result close to the observed value of the target since the model was constructed to represent these observations as accurately as possible. However, strictly speaking, it would be even more interesting to construct models that are valid also outside the observed sample – that is, which can be generalized to a wider population (e.g., Singapore children in general and not only those included in the sample). To get an idea about the predictive power of a model beyond the sample used for model construction, statisticians have used different kinds of so-called resampling methods for nearly 60 years (cf., e.g., Lachenbruch & Mickey 1968 for leave-one-out crossvalidation, Efron 1979 for the bootstrap method, Politis et al. 1999 for subsampling).

In resampling, a random part of the observed sample is excluded from model construction, and for this so-called hold out the predictive power is tested by the comparison of the predicted and observed values of the target. By repeated resampling, it is ensured that each part of the overall sample is part of at least one hold out so that a measure of predictive power can be constructed based on the overall sample of observations.

In our PrInDT approach, we slightly adapt this procedure for the construction of optimal models. Typically, repeated resampling leads to many different models representing the relationship between target and predictors. The entirety of such models is traditionally referred as "ensemble." In statistics, such ensembles are generally used for model assessment. In our approach, we employ ensembles to identify the best tree according to a problem-adequate accuracy criterion to be introduced in detail in Section 4.1.

Another important aspect to consider when looking for models with high predictive power is the danger of so-called overfitting of the training set (i.e., a too-perfect fit on the training set that makes the generalization of results to other parts of the population difficult). It is, therefore, of crucial importance to avoid overfitting (i.e., to generate models with high predictive power; cf. Section 4.3 for further comments on avoiding overfitting).

3.2.7 Two-Stage and Interdependent Models

Let us, finally, introduce two more advanced statistical modeling techniques used in linguistics, which motivate our approach. The approach called **MuPDAR(F)** (Multifactorial Prediction and Deviation Analysis using Regression/Random Forests), introduced by Gries (2022), distinguishes two kinds of speakers: the reference speakers (RSs), which are employed for constructing a first model, and the target speakers on which the first model is tested. MuPDAR(F) involves four steps:

i. A regression or classification model is estimated for the reference speakers (RSs).

ii. If this first model is good (enough), the target variable is predicted for the target speakers (TSs).
iii. The TSs' actual target value is compared to the prediction of the first model.
iv. A second model is estimated with a response indicating the correctness of the prediction of the first model. The response may be either binary (prediction correctly or not) or numerical (probability of the correct TSs' choice estimated by the first model in case of classification or by the difference of actual and predicted values in case of regression). The second model uses the same predictors as the first model but with the corresponding values of the TSs.

This kind of modeling includes two estimation stages (i and iv). This way, the properties of the TSs leading to deviation of the observed target values from the prediction by the first model can be confirmed by the second model. This is extremely valuable for analyses where two groups of speakers are compared, since differences between the behavior of the two groups can be revealed. Two-stage modeling is also one of the ideas of our PrInDT approach for estimating interdependent models (see Sections 4.5.6 and 5.6; for an application, see Section 5.4.2).

Studies investigating the interdependencies of particular features are extremely rare in linguistics. One exception is Larsson et al. (2021), who discuss the great potential of interdependent models for corpus linguistics. However, in most studies of varieties of English, characteristics are investigated in isolation and either listed as sets of particular features in overview collections of World Englishes (e.g., Kortmann et al. 2020 and the two edited volumes by Kortmann et al. 2004 and Schneider et al. 2004) or as individual studies. The relationship between, say, the realization of local phonological features and morphosyntactic features (i.e., the question whether a speaker who makes strong use of local phonological features also strongly employs local grammatical characteristics) is underresearched so far. Interdependent models enable testing hypotheses of relationships between multiple dependent and independent variables. In their application, Larsson et al. (2021) focused on whether the dependent variables for their research question are influenced solely by the independent variables or whether they also influence each other. This is a common question for studies with more than one dependent variable. A typical modeling approach is a combination of linear models, referred to as "structural equation models," as in the R-package lavaan (Rosseel 2012) used in Larsson et al (2021). Our PrInDT approach offers an alternative for the investigation of interdependencies between classification and regression models by means of optimized decision trees. In particular, we consider whether the dependent variables are influenced solely by the independent variables or whether they also influence each other (cf. Section 4.5.6).

4 PrInDT: Prediction and Interpretation of Decision Trees

As discussed in the preceding sections, this Element of World Englishes aims to address the shortcomings of many current statistical approaches used in linguistics and, in particular, in World Englishes research (cf. Sections 1–3). We exclusively employ and discuss decision trees since they are easy and straightforward to interpret, in particular when compared to other models such as mixed-effects models. As already addressed in Section 3.2.3.3, decision trees are easy to plot and their graphic representations illustrate so-called if-then rules that are intuitive and straightforward to interpret. Understanding mixed-effects models requires various kinds of plots for the interpretation of effects and predictor dependencies (cf. Section 3.2.3.1). We further focus on ctrees (Hothorn et al. 2006) since the size of these trees can be easily controlled by the specification of a significance level (cf. Section 3.2.3.3). In our PrInDT approach (Weihs & Buschfeld 2021a, 2021b, 2021c), we aim to identify the best ctree from a variety of potential trees generated by different resampling methods. As the accuracy criterion, we always employ the balanced accuracy for classification and R^2 for regression on the full sample (cf. Section 4.1).

Looking through textbooks on statistics for linguists, it is striking that regression models are intensively discussed in all of them. Decision trees are commonly used, in particular in variationist linguistics (cf. Tagliamonte & Baayen 2012) and mentioned in the books by Levshina (2015) and Gries (2021). However, how to identify optimal trees (i.e., the option of comparing individual trees and selecting the best one) is never really dealt with. Instead, ensembles like random forests are proposed for the assessment of variable importance at the expense of interpretability since many trees cannot really be interpreted together because the interaction of the full set of "if-then rules" in many different trees is very difficult to assess. Furthermore, we saw in preliminary pilot investigations that single trees might exist that have an even higher predictive power than their ensembles. This might be due to the fact that ensembles generally also include trees with low accuracy, which decrease the overall accuracy of the whole ensemble. Thus, in what follows, we will mainly focus on individual ctrees.

4.1 Model Selection: Accuracy Revisited

In linguistics, ctrees are commonly determined based on the full set of the observed data, and in classification their accuracy is estimated without taking into account the different sizes of the classes (cf. Section 3.2.4). To avoid models that underpredict the smaller class and improve the generalizability of trees (i.e., the validity of their results beyond the observed data and thus for a wider [speech] community), we have developed the PrInDT approach for both classification and regression models (cf. Section 3.2.3).

Model selection is an important task in statistics. The main discussion revolves around how to weigh complexity/interpretability of a model against its accuracy. A well-known simple measure for complexity is the length of a model (Rissanen 1978) measured, for example, by the number of coefficients in a linear model or the number of nodes in a decision tree. The question is how large, and thus complex, we would want a model to become to improve its accuracy, at the expense of straightforward interpretation. This question relates to the notion of overfitting of models – that is, which fit too closely or even exactly to their training data, so that they cannot make accurate predictions on any data other than the training data.

In our PrInDT approach, we decided to weigh accuracy and interpretability against each other and optimize the accuracy of models still keeping them small enough and thus easy to interpret. For ctrees, it is reasonably easy to restrict model size by means of an external parameter, namely the maximum significance level of a split (cf. Section 3.2.3.3). In most of our analyses, it appeared to be adequate to set this level to 1%. For models with this maximum significance level, we then aim for optimizing their accuracy. However, it needs to be kept in mind that for a higher maximum significance level (e.g., 5%), accuracies might be higher but may lead to overfitting. For a more detailed discussion of how to avoid overfitting, see Section 4.3.

Concerning the accuracy of classification models, we decided to adapt the measure of overall accuracy (cf. Section 3.2.4) so that the small classes are more prominently and realistically considered. We, therefore, aim to identify the best tree by building trees on many random subsamples of the observed data and assess their accuracy on the full sample by means of so-called balanced accuracies. By measuring accuracy on the full sample, our accuracy measure assesses not only the accuracy on the part of the sample used for model construction (training sample) but also the accuracy on the unused part (test sample). Since the accuracy on the test sample is assessed, too, our accuracy measure at least partly assesses the generalizability of predictions (discussed in Section 3.2.6), in contrast to accuracy measures for models that use the full sample for training.

Balanced accuracies are averages of the individual accuracies of the different classes investigated, for example, for two classes:

balanced accuracy = ((accuracy in class 1) + (accuracy in class 2))/2.

As already mentioned in Section 1, in a binary classification analysis of sociolinguistic data, we often have a large and a small class, represented by a "standard" linguistic realization (e.g., *realized* subject pronouns) and a non-standard, locally, or socially bound realization (e.g., *zero* subjects), respectively. By calculating the accuracies of both classes individually and using their average, the small class is adequately considered. This is often not the case when measuring "standard" accuracies since the two classes are not distinguished in the calculation (cf. Section 3.2.4).

In our approach for classification, we use balanced accuracies since in classification models as introduced in Sections 3.2.3.2 and 3.2.3.3 the accuracy in one class is (close to) 1 and in the other (close to) 0. This is reflected by balanced accuracies of 0.52 and 0.50, respectively.

In regression, we utilize the (standard) R^2 measure to assess model accuracy (cf. Section 3.2.4.1), again calculated using the full sample.

4.2 Restrictions on Trees

When aiming to identify decision trees that represent the interplay between dependent and independent variables in a data set most adequately, we sometimes generated trees including splits that contradicted expectations based on earlier and often long-standing and empirically tested linguistic assumptions. This left us with two options of interpretation: Assume that either prior theoretical assumptions were wrong or the respective tree(s) accidentally split the data according to a biased sample. Working with such a tree, however, might lead to wrongly motivated reconsiderations of long-standing theoretical approaches (cf. Section 3.2.5). We therefore decided to aim for a statistical solution to this problem. It should be noted here again that we always build more than one tree, often a thousand, and would strongly advise against just selecting the first tree R might generate, in particular since this might generate accidental chance findings not representing linguistic realities. If we opt for generating, for example, 999 trees on the basis of the subsampling procedure introduced in Section 3.2.6, we get a wide selection of trees with often similar accuracies. On the one hand, this allows us to identify the tree with the best accuracy possible. On the other hand, we can compare the number of trees that display unexpected results against the number of trees which correspond to prior theoretical assumptions and/or our hypotheses-driven expectations. To this end, we added an analytical step to the PrInDT program that excludes trees that contain such unexpected or uninterpretable splits. In our application (cf. Section 5.1.1), such splits have normally been in the clear minority and could thus be interpreted as accidental results not to be given too much attention. However, if such unexpected splits turned out to be very frequent, let alone in the majority, one would have to reconsider prior theoretical assumptions and/or reject one's hypotheses. Therefore, by considering the proportion of excluded trees in relation to the general number of generated trees (e.g., 999, to be set by the user), we can verify the reliability of statistical models as well as earlier theoretical approaches. Furthermore, the interpretability of trees is improved since we no longer have to struggle with statistical output we cannot interpret (cf. Section 5.1.1 for an application).

As an example for such restrictions, we, once again, refer to the study on subject-pronoun realization (cf. Section 2.1.1). According to theoretical, language typological considerations, the ethnicity groups *E/a* (England ancestral) and *S/C* (Singapore Chinese) should behave differently when it comes to the realization (or omission) of subject pronouns. Since bilingual language acquisition, as found in most Singaporean children, is strongly guided by crosslinguistic influence (i.e., the influence of one language on the other when simultaneously acquired), language pairings such as English/Chinese might lead to structures different from British and American English (BrE/AmE) standards. Chinese is a null-subject language (i.e., a language that does not always require an overt subject; for details, cf. Valian 2016: 388). This may encourage the omission of subjects by children simultaneously acquiring English and Chinese, in particular since this is what the children also find in the English input they receive from their parents; zero subjects have been attested as a feature of SingE in various earlier studies on the L2 variety.

As another example, also related to the realization of subject pronouns, children with MLU=1 (the younger children in the participant cohort) can be expected to behave quite differently from children with MLU=3 (the older share of participants), since zero subject pronouns are a feature of early language acquisition, also in children acquiring BrE/AmE (Roeper & Rohrbacher 2000, among many others). Therefore, we would not expect these two groups to cluster together against MLU=2 (the middle-aged children in the cohort) if MLU turned out as a significant split.

We employ the following specification in PrInDT to exclude unexpected combinations:

```
ctestv <- rbind('ETH == {E/a, S/C}','ETH == {E/a,E/m,S/C}','ETH == {E/a,E/migr,S/C}',
         'ETH == {E/a,E/m,E/migr,S/C}','ETH == {E/a,E/m,E/migr,S/C,S/I}',
         'ETH == {E/a,E/m,E/migr,S/C,S/m}','ETH == {E/a,E/m,S/C,S/I}',
         'ETH == {E/a,E/migr,S/C,S/I}','ETH == {E/a,S/C,S/I}','MLU == {1,3}')
```

In this code, the function rbind (row-bind) builds a (row-)vector from the entries separated by commas. In ctestv (conditions-to-test-vector), all split results are specified that should not be included in the trees (separated by commas); in our example, all split results in which the combinations {*E/a, S/C*} for ETH and {1,3} for MLU (== means "equal to") appear. Such restrictions are easy to define and put into practice for models like decision trees that make decisions on the basis of individual predictors.

4.3 Optimization of Decision Trees

The main idea of PrInDT is the optimization of the accuracy of decision trees – whether an exclusion of potentially misleading trees is needed prior to this or not strongly depends on the respective investigation and data set. The general procedure for modeling decision trees is to construct each individual split to optimally separate the observations in the corresponding subparts (cf. Section 3.2.3.3). This can be considered a "local" optimization since for each split the optimal decision is made. However, for the complete tree, accuracy is not optimized. Even worse, the accuracy of the complete tree is not considered during tree construction.

The idea behind our approach is to look for decisions trees that "globally" optimize the accuracy on the full sample. This is implemented by constructing the trees on random subsamples, calculating their accuracies on the full sample and comparing these accuracies with each other, and selecting the tree with the highest accuracy on the full sample.

In order to identify the best tree, we adapt and combine ideas from bagging (bootstrap aggregating), bumping (bootstrap umbrella of model parameters), and random forests (cf. Hastie et al. 2008: 282, 290, 587). To assess true prediction, we employ subsampling and not bootstrap sampling, as in bagging, in order to avoid multiple entries of observations in the training sample. Bootstrap sampling works "with replacement"; after an element has been selected for a sample, it is "put back" so that it can be selected again. This way, multiple entries of the same observations can appear in the training sample. Subsampling works "without replacement"; once an element has been selected for a sample, it cannot be selected again. We decided that multiple entries of the same observation in the training sample are not sensible since multiple entries would introduce weights on the observations. Both resampling approaches, with and without replacement, are designed to account for overfitting since both approaches come with test sets on which the predictive power can be tested (cf., e.g., Strobl et al. 2024). Since our training sample should represent random selections of, for example, speakers and tokens, we decided for subsampling to exclude multiple inclusions of the same observation.

As in random forests, we not only use subsamples of the observations but also subsamples of the predictors for the individual trees. However, we simplify the procedure by drawing the subsample of the predictors only once for each tree and not again and again for each node of each tree (cf. Ho 1998).

As in bagging, we construct many trees, a so-called ensemble of trees, on random subsamples of the observations. In bagging, the mean predictive power of all trees in the ensemble is considered. In contrast, in bumping and in the PrInDT approach, we look for the tree in the ensemble of trees that comes with the best accuracy for the full data set; our motivation is to focus on just one (best) tree (cf. Section 4).

The method of bumping is called as such (i.e., "Bootstrap umbrella of model parameters"), since it makes use of bootstrap sampling for generating an ensemble in which the best tree is identified (Tibshirani & Knight 1999). Since we use subsampling instead of bootstrap sampling, we call our method "sumping" (subsampling umbrella of model parameters).

Other optimization methods aim to find optimal decision trees that are directly constructed on the full sample without subsampling. For special kinds of trees, for example, CORELS (Certifiable Optimal RulE ListS) is a discrete optimization technique for building rule lists over a categorical feature space. This algorithm provides the optimal solution for binary predictors (Angelino et al. 2018). The optimality is theoretically guaranteed, though only for binary predictors.

For the general case of classification and regression trees, the evtree method (Grubinger et al. 2014) aims to find the optimal tree by means of so-called evolutionary algorithms where, given an initial tree, improved solutions are searched through stochastic changes to the tree structure.

Both algorithms, CORELS and evtree, ignore the problem of bad predictive power for small classes, though, and do not allow for interpretability restrictions. Hence, they do not consider undersampling or the use of balanced accuracies in tree construction. In the PrInDT approach we, therefore, do not build on evtree but on bumping, which allows for restrictions, too.

In PrInDT, one main idea is to find the model that best generalizes to tokens not used for model building. To this end, we only use subsamples of our original sample for model construction and test the model on the tokens that are not selected for the subsample to assess the generalizability of the model. In PrInDT, we decided to assess model quality on the whole sample so that we can directly compare models based on different subsamples. Therefore, our criterion combines goodness of model fit for the subsample used for model construction and predictive power for the rest of the overall sample.

We offer different methods for subsampling. The overall best model is identified by comparing the quality of the best models found by the different subsampling methods. For binary classification, we employ the following subsampling methods:

1. The basic idea is to randomly "undersample" the large class so that in model construction the large class has a similar number of tokens as the small class. To achieve this, the percentages of tokens to be included in the subsamples can be specified, typically a high percentage for the small class and a small percentage for the large class. The PrInDT functions **PrInDT**, **RePrInDT**, and **OptPrInDT** use this kind of subsampling (cf. Section 4.5.1).
2. Furthermore, we have developed a function of PrInDT that is geared toward resampling imbalanced data sets concerning comparisons of groups of speakers of different sizes. To this end, we first randomly select the same number of speakers from each group (in our case Singaporean and English children) and afterwards randomly undersample the large class. This way, we balance not only the classes but also the number of participants in each group to be compared (cf. function **PrInDTCstruc** in Section 4.5.1).

Please keep in mind that our subsampling for model construction does not result in disregarding the tokens that were not chosen for model building. Our subsampling methods only aim to find the most representative subsample that best generalizes to the whole sample so that for the assessment of model quality all tokens are considered.

For regression, the percentage of the tokens in the subsample employed for model construction can be specified (cf. function **PrInDTreg** in Section 4.5.4) and also structured subsampling of the children is offered (cf. function **PrInDTRstruc** in Section 4.5.4). In both, classification and regression, the percentage of features employed for model construction can be varied, too.

All these ideas are included in the software package PrInDT, which is available in R (Weihs & Buschfeld 2025; R Core Team 2019). In this Element, we provide a detailed description of some of the ideas utilized by the approach for the first time. In the following parts of this section, we introduce all functions of the R-package PrInDT developed by the second author. In Section 5, we illustrate how they work through applications to World Englishes data sets, which were collected by the first author, as described in Section 2. In Section 5, we compare the best models generated by the different PrInDT functions to identify the best model for each application.

4.4 Data Preparation for PrInDT

For using the PrInDT package, we first have to prepare a data frame in R containing all relevant target and predictor variables. All variables in this data frame will be utilized for the analysis. Variables that might be part of the data set but are not needed for the actual analysis need to be eliminated:

```
CHILDzero <- datachild$CHILD # extraction of children data
data <- datachild[,-1] # elimination of CHILD from data frame
data <- na.omit(data) # elimination of missings
```

In this example, the stored data set was read into the data frame datachild (cf. Section 3.1). From this data frame, the variable CHILD is eliminated since it should not be used as a predictor in the PrInDT analysis. In addition, if missing values in observations exist (e.g., if the age of a child is not known), these observations are eliminated.

PrInDT functions have a number of inputs, only some of which have a standard value called default, which is preset in the system. Inputs without defaults need to be specified according to the given needs of an analysis. In the following discussion, we introduce all inputs of the basic function **PrInDT**. The first two inputs are the data set to be processed and the target variable. They can be specified by their names as the first two entries in the list of inputs: PrInDT(data,"real", . . .). The next input, ctestv, representing the vector of conditions to be tested (cf. Section 4.2) has the default NA (= not available = no restrictions). This input only needs to be specified if restrictions in the splits of the trees are required (cf. Section 4.2). **PrInDT** also employs the number of replications N and the percentages of the large and the small class (percl, percs; cf. Section 4.3), as well as the confidence level conf.level = mincriterion = (1 − maximum significance level; cf. Section 3.2.3.3). These inputs also have defaults, namely N=99, conf.level=0.95, percs=1, and percl= (no. of tokens in the small class)/(no. of tokens in the large class), so that the larger class has the same number of tokens as the small class in the subsamples. These inputs can be modified according to the respective needs of individual analyses by assigning their value to the name of the input in the list of inputs (e.g., N=999). If we want to use the same value of N for different applications, we can also specify this before application, for example, by Nall <- 999, and assign the variable name in the list of inputs, for example N=Nall. We typically first try out the default settings and then aim to improve our results by specifying other values for N, percl, percs, and conf.level, as in the second call of the PrInDT function in the following example. In the following sections, the values we present for the inputs are the results of trying out different values to gain the best possible models. Here are two examples for an application of **PrInDT**:

```
out <- PrInDT(data,"real") # minimum specifications, when all defaults should be used
Nall <- 999
# ctestv specified before, e.g., as in Section 4.2
out <- PrInDT(data,"real",ctestv=ctestv,N=Nall,percl=0.08,percs=0.95,conf.level=0.99)
```

The output of the function is assigned to the list out. We can print the results stored in out by the statement print(out) or directly by typing out. We can plot results by plot(out). If we want to print or plot a specific result only, we can use the $-notation, for example, plot(out$tree1st) or print(out$tree1st) for the best (first) tree found. Each PrInDT function has a specific presentation of results. For further details and examples of possible outputs of PrInDT functions, consider the help function, which can be accessed (e.g., for the basic function **PrInDT**) via help(PrInDT).

4.5 The Functions of the PrInDT Package

4.5.1 Two-Class Classification

The basic function **PrInDT** of the package originally introduced in Weihs and Buschfeld (2021a) enhances the functionality of ctrees for a two-class classification problem (i.e., for a classification problem with two categories, as in the case of the *subpro* data set where the dependent variable "subject pronoun realization" has the two classes *realized* and *zero*). In this example, the two classes have very different sizes. The class *zero* comprises less than 9% of the data sample, and the class *realized* contains more than 91% of the data. In such a situation, model building takes the larger class into account much more frequently than the smaller one, and as a consequence, the smaller class is often never, or at least far too seldom, predicted by the model. This has been discussed in Section 3.2.4. For such data sets, we use so-called undersampling of the large class (here *realized*) to balance the classes for model building. This means that for the subsamples, we choose a much smaller percentage of the large class than the small class (cf. the R-code in Section 4.4 for an example).

The aim is to identify the ideal combination of subsampling percentages of the two classes for model building. The function **RePrInDT** (originally proposed in Weihs & Buschfeld 2021c) analyzes each pair of percentages from prespecified lists of percentages of the small and large classes, and identifies the pair of percentages that yields the best model. The function **OptPrInDT** can then explore adjacent percentages of the best percentages identified by **RePrInDT** to find an even-better model.

For the identification of the best model, the function **PrInDT** uses random subsampling from all tokens/observations. As an alternative, the function **PrInDTCstruc** offers so-called structured subsampling. For this, we assume that an underlying substructure exists in the data from which we can sample first. An example for such a substructure are the children represented in our *subpro* data set. These are further divided into two different categories (i.e., Singapore and England). Samples are taken using the following method: First, subsampling from the elements of the substructure is carried out so that the two categories Singapore and England appear with equal frequency. Second, on the data of the randomly chosen elements of the substructure, undersampling can be applied for balancing the classes of the target variable (e.g., *realized* and *zero* for subject-pronoun realization).

If elements of the underlying substructure (e.g., the observed individuals) do not exhibit both target classes but only one, the procedure is restricted to the first stage (i.e., to randomly selecting elements of the substructure). In **PrInDTCstruc**, we employ the substructure for identifying a "representative" subset of elements (here individuals) that best covers the complete variation in that it generates the model with the best accuracy. Concerning prediction, we simply assume that so far unobserved elements do not add further variance to the target, which is a standard assumption in prediction by statistical models.

Additionally, subsampling of predictors is implemented for classification in the PrInDT package. We offer four different versions of structured subsampling in **PrInDTCstruc** – namely,

a. subsampling just of the elements in the substructure,
b. subsampling just of the predictors,
c. first subsampling of the predictors and then, in the resulting subset, subsampling of the elements of the substructure, and
d. first subsampling of the elements of the substructure and then, in the resulting subset, subsampling of the predictors.

For classification problems, undersampling is applied unless specified otherwise by undersamp="FALSE". The provided versions of structured subsampling are specified by means of vers="a" to vers="d". For an application of this method to the *subpro* data set, see Section 5.1.2.

4.5.2 Nested Resampling

An imbalance in the data may also be caused by one of the predictors, for example, if the token frequency of one class (variant) of a predictor strongly differs from the other (e.g., 20 female versus 500 male participants in a study investigating linguistic differences between male and female speakers). In such cases, the more frequent category tends to dominate model building (i.e., it is chosen relatively more often than the less frequent category).

To balance the influence of the categories of such a predictor in model building, the PrInDT function **NesPrInDT** (originally proposed in Weihs & Buschfeld 2021b) allows for the additional subsampling of one of the predictors for two-class classification. This is applied to the *nessubpro* data set, which contains both the child data from *subpro* as well as data from adult speakers from the ICE-Singapore (cf. Section 2.1.2). In this example, the overall data set is characterized by an imbalance of 3,225 tokens from the children and 17,325 tokens from the adults, which is subsampled to balance the number of adult and child tokens. This leads to so-called nested subsampling of the predictor (here, speaker) and the categorical dependent variable (here, pronoun realization). First, balanced subsets of the predictor are built. In a next step, we then balance the classes of the dependent variable. For each of the subsets with balanced classes in each subset of the predictor, a PrInDT model is built. Finally, the function identifies the best of these models overall. For an application of these ideas, see Section 5.2.

4.5.3 Multiclass Classification

So far, we have treated two-class problems only. For dependent categorical variables with more than two classes, the function **PrInDTMulev** was developed. This is applied to the *past* data set with the three categories *marked*, *unmarked*, and *finish*, as introduced in Section 2.1.3. For such tasks, we employ the so-called one-versus-rest strategy of classification: We apply the basic function **PrInDT** for two-class classification individually to each of the classes in comparison to a joint treatment of the remaining classes. This way, we get individual classification models for the distinction of the individual classes from the joint treatment of the other classes (i.e., we learn how individual classes differ from the other classes). For each observation of the full sample, the models for the individual classes deliver the probability of the corresponding class. Finally, the class with the highest probability is chosen as the predicted class for the observation. For an application of this procedure to the *past* data set, see Section 5.3.

4.5.4 Regression

All the functions described in Sections 4.5.1 to 4.5.3 have been constructed for classification problems (i.e., for problems with a categorical dependent variable). In contrast, the function **PrInDTreg** has been developed for regression problems with a continuous dependent variable. As an example, this function is applied to the *vowel* data set to compare the vowel lengths of words in the two lexical sets KIT and FLEECE, as produced by Singaporean and English children (cf. Section 2.1.4).

PrInDTreg utilizes random subsampling of all tokens/observations. The function **PrInDTRstruc** offers structured subsampling for regression with the same versions a through d as in **PrInDTCstruc** (cf. Section 4.5.1). Additional undersampling of classes is not possible, since responses are not categorical but continuous. For an application of these approaches, see Section 5.4.

4.5.5 Multilabel Classification

Furthermore, PrInDT provides functions for data with more than one binary factor label (i.e., for data with more than one categorical binary dependent variable). These functions are applied to the landscape data set *land* introduced in Section 2.2. Our investigation focuses on building models for three dependent variables – namely, the use of the three different languages, Dutch, English, and French, on St. Martin signs. As independent predictors, we employ different properties of language use on official signage, as introduced in Section 2.2.

Our approach is motivated by Probst et al. (2017) but differs with respect to the data set used for estimation. Whereas Probst and colleagues model the full data set, our PrInDT approach aims to identify the best model on the basis of random subsamples along two subsequent stages of analysis. At stage 1, for each individual target (i.e., each individual language), we base the model on the independent predictors only. At stage 2, we also investigate how the targets influence each other, in addition to the independent predictors.

In the function **PrInDTMulab**, models that are exclusively based on the independent predictors are called stage 1 or BR (Binary Relevance) models. Models also estimated by means of the other dependent variables are called stage 2 or DBR (Dependent Binary Relevance) models. The BR models calculate predicted values of the dependent variables. These predictions are then used instead of the originally observed values of the dependent variables in the DBR models, and new predictions are determined by the DBR models. The latter approach is called DBRT (Dependent Binary Relevance with True predictions).

In our application, the models for the three languages are combined to predict which of the three languages appear on a sign. Since we have more than one dependent variable, we also employ (multilabel) accuracy measures taking into account all predictions of all models. We assess the accuracy of these predictions in three ways: The first measure considers the share of signs for which all three languages are correctly predicted (01-accuracy); the second measure provides the share of correct predictions of the individual languages (Hamming accuracy; both measures adapted from Probst et al. 2017). Since both measures do not distinguish the two classes of the targets (e.g., English on the sign or not), we also use the mean of the balanced accuracies for the three languages as a third measure. All these multilabel measures are used to assess the BR, DBR, and DBRT predictions. For DBRT, the measures characterize the predictive power of the independent predictors on the basis of the stage 2 models. For an application of **PrInDTMulab**, see Section 5.5.

4.5.6 Interdependent Models

For multilabel classification by means of DBR, we employed a so-called interdependent classification model, in which the dependent variables may also depend on each other (cf. Section 4.5.5). This means, for example, that we assume that the use of one language on a sign might also depend on the use of one or more of the other languages. However, interdependent models can also be used for continuous dependent variables and even for models in which both categorical and continuous dependent variables are included.

In accordance with Larsson et al. (2021; cf. Section 3.2.7), we argue that interdependent analyses of linguistic aspects, be they linguistic features of speech production or language use on signs, might yield important, so far widely neglected, insights into the overall sociolinguistic situation of a territory and the dependency of such aspects on each other. We may, for example, want to test the dependency between subject-pronoun realization and past-tense marking to see whether speakers who make frequent use of one local feature also have a strong inclination toward the use of other local characteristics. We may further want to predict the realization of subject pronouns of a person in a particular speech context based on the percentage of nonstandard past-tense marking of this same person. These ideas are implemented in PrInDT and make the approach particularly relevant since the realization of individual linguistic characteristics might not be independent of each other.

In so-called simultaneous models, two or more target variables are modeled in dependence of each other and other predictors. The target variables are called dependent variables or "endogenous variables." The predictors that are not endogenous are called independent variables or "exogenous variables." The idea of simultaneous/interdependent models is that realizations of the dependent variables may not only depend on realizations of the independent variables but also on those of the other dependent variables.

In Section 3.2.7, we already introduced the idea that in an analysis with more than one dependent variable, we have to consider whether the dependent variables are influenced solely by the independent variables or whether they also influence each other (for a linguistic example; cf. Larsson et al. 2021).

Therefore, in the following discussion, we distinguish two different approaches for interdependent modeling. In the first approach (*Exo-approach*), we assume that only the values of the exogenous variables are available to model the endogenous variables. In this approach, interdependency is limited to the usage of predictions of the endogenous variables from the exogenous variables as predictors additional to the exogenous variables. For so-far-unobserved values of the exogenous variables, such models can directly predict the endogenous variables. In the second approach (*Endo-approach*), we assume that the values of all variables are directly available for model building so that we can model the endogenous variables on the basis of both the exogenous and other endogenous variables. Such models can be used, for example, for unveiling the relationships between the endogenous variables.

The function **PrInDTMulab** described in Section 4.5.5 is a mixture of the two approaches. In **PrInDTMulab**, the endogenous variables are modeled in two ways: based on the exogenous variables only and on the basis of both the exogenous and the observed endogenous variables. In a final step, the predictions from the model on the exogenous variables are inserted into the model, which is based on both exogenous and endogenous variables, and predictions are calculated again.

4.5.6.1 The *Exo-approach*

In the first approach, the *Exo-approach*, we distinguish the following two stages of modeling: At stage 1, each endogenous variable is modeled exclusively in dependence on the exogenous variables. To find the best model, the corresponding PrInDT function (**PrInDT** for two-class classification, **PrInDTMulev** for multiclass classification, and **PrInDTreg** for regression) is applied. By means of the resulting models, the values of the endogenous variables are predicted. At stage 2, each endogenous variable is remodeled in dependence of the predictions of the other endogenous variables and the exogenous variables. Once again, the corresponding PrInDT function is applied to identify the best model.

This kind of method was invented more than 50 years ago for least squares estimation. The so-called 2SLS (2 Stage Least Squares) method, for which least-squares estimation is used instead of decision-tree modeling, is ascribed to Theil (1971). We just adapted the method for decision trees.

4.5.6.2 The *Endo-approach*

In the second approach, the *Endo-approach*, all exogenous and endogenous variables are used as predictors. We also proceed in two stages: At stage 1, we base the model on the full sample; the accuracy of the resulting model is used as a reference value. At stage 2, we try to improve the model from stage 1 by using structured subsampling (cf. Sections 4.5.1 and 4.5.4). At stage 2, we distinguish two subapproaches. In the *EndoI-approach* (Endogenous Individual), we apply structured resampling individually for each endogenous variable (i.e., we optimize the models of the individual endogenous variables independent of the other models). This way, the best models found for the different endogenous variables are based on different sets of elements of the substructure (e.g., children) and/or predictors. In contrast, in the *EndoJ-approach* (Endogenous Joint), we identify those elements of the substructure and/or those predictors that fit best for a joint construction of all endogenous variables. This is achieved by optimizing the mean accuracy over all endogenous variables using the same set of elements and/or predictors for all endogenous variables. By the *EndoJ-approach*, the nonselected elements of the substructure and/or the nonselected predictors are ignored for model building overall. However, because the same elements and predictors have to be used for the construction of all models, model accuracies may be lower in the *EndoJ-approach* than in the *EndoI-approach*.

4.5.6.3 Three Kinds of Simultaneous Models

In both the *Exo-* and the *Endo-approach*, we distinguish three types of simultaneous models. The first type (type I) are classification models, in which all endogenous variables represent discrete classes/categories, all variables are observed for the same entities, and all endogenous variables depend on the same exogenous variables. The second type (type II) are regression *models*, which have the same structure as type I models, but the endogenous variables represent continuous measurements. Finally, type III models are *joint classification and regression models*, in which the endogenous variables can be discrete/categorical or continuous. Here, we allow for different sets of observed objects (e.g., subject pronouns, past-tense marking, and vowel length) and different sets of elements in the substructure (e.g., combinations of participants, for which the different endogenous variables are observed, as well as different sets of exogenous variables), which are used to model the different endogenous variables.

For type III, since different sets of objects may be observed for the different endogenous variables, and even the participants of a study who contributed speech for analysis may be different for the different endogenous variables, it is to be expected that not all endogenous variables are observed for all objects. That is the reason why we first summarize the predictions of the endogenous variables determined at stage 1 for each participant to prepare stage 2 of modeling. These summaries are percentages (per person) for discrete variables and means (per person) for continuous variables. At stage 2, the values of these summaries are used as additional predictors for all observations of the element of the substructure, for which the summary measure was calculated. If a summary is needed for a person for which an endogenous variable is not observed, the mean of all calculated summaries of this variable is used as the summary.

For the first approach, for each of the provided modeling types I, II, III, specific PrInDT functions are available: for example, **C2SPrInDT** (Two-Stage Classification) for models of type I, **R2SPrInDT** (Two-Stage Regression) for models of type II, and **Mix2SPrInDT** (Two-Stage Classification-Regression Mix) for models of type III. For the second approach, the corresponding PrInDT functions are **SimCPrInDT** for classification for models of type I, **SimRPrInDT** for regression for models of type II, and **SimMixPrInDT** for a classification-regression mix for models of type III. For applications of these functions, see Section 5.6.

5 PrInDT Applications in World Englishes

As already described in Section 2, we have developed the PrInDT approach on the basis of World Englishes data from Singapore, England, and the Caribbean island of St. Martin. In the following section, we apply three different classification tasks to these data: For the Singapore and England data, we consider two-class classification of subject-pronoun realization (cf. Sections 2.1.1 and 2.1.2) and three-class classification of past-tense marking (cf. Section 2.1.3). The St. Martin data are analyzed by means of multilabel classification of the usage frequencies and types of different language-usage patterns on public signs (cf. Section 2.2). For regression, we apply our method to the prediction of vowel lengths (cf. Section 2.1.4).

5.1 Subject-Pronoun Realization: Two-Class Classification Trees

For the *subpro* data set introduced in Section 2.1.1, we aim to determine whether any of the independent variables has a statistically significant influence on subject-pronoun realization in Singapore and England. Since we have a target variable with two (very unbalanced) classes, we apply two-class classification modeling (cf. Section 4.5.1).

The data set used for the following analysis was already analyzed by means of logistic regression and decision trees in Buschfeld (2020: 178, 179); some first results have also been presented in Sections 3.2.3.2 and 3.2.3.3. In these analyses, only the overall accuracy (cf. Section 3.2.4) was discussed. In Buschfeld and Weihs (2024), the PrInDT idea was already applied to this data set but without restricting the trees. Restrictions, as introduced in Section 4.2, were only applied in the papers, in which the PrInDT idea was introduced (cf. Weihs & Buschfeld 2021a, 2021c). In the following, we introduce the two possible PrInDT options for analyzing the *subpro* data set (i.e., modeling by random subsampling and modeling by structured subsampling).

5.1.1 Modeling by Random Subsampling

In the following sections, for each PrInDT function we first introduce the R-code we employ for our analysis, before we report the results and the model generated by the respective function. In this section, all functions of the PrInDT package used for modeling the *subpro* data set datazero are called up via the target "real", with the restrictions ctestv on specific combinations of levels (e.g., Singapore Chinese versus English ancestral children; cf. Section 4.2), and the confidence level conf.level=0.99. For the function **PrInDT**, the variable CHILD has been eliminated from the data frame datazero, as demonstrated in Section 4.4. The variable CHILD represents a stochastic effect, which we only consider via the function **PrInDTCstruc** introduced in Section 5.1.2. For the percentages of the small and large classes, percs and percl, defaults exist, namely percs=1 (i.e., the choice of the full small class) and percl so that the large class has the same size as the small class in the simulations. We tried this combination of percentages and the alternative percl=0.08, percs=0.95. The latter was the best combination of percentages with respect to balanced accuracy we found at that stage of modeling. In this combination of percentages, the size of the smaller class corresponds to 502 tokens and the size of the larger class corresponds to 449 tokens in the subsamples (i.e., in the subsamples, the smaller class is even slightly better represented than the larger class). In what follows, we always try to choose an optimal combination of percentages (cf. Section 4.4). The R-code appears as follows:

```
# datazero = subpro data after elimination of CHILD
N <- 999 # number of repetitions
outdef <- PrInDT(datazero,"real",ctestv,N=N,conf.level=0.99) # percentages=defaults
print(outdef) # standard output
out <- PrInDT(datazero,"real",ctestv,N=N,percl=0.08,percs=0.95,conf.level=0.99)
print(out)
plot(out$tree1st) # plot of best tree on full sample
```

When we turn to the results, we see that the best model for the combination percl=0.094 and percs=1 has a balanced accuracy of 0.7025. The best model (tree1st) generated by the alternative combination percl=0.08, percs=0.95 has a slightly higher balanced accuracy of 0.7033. This tree is shown in Figure 5. For this combination of percentages, 944 of the 999 repetitions were accepted,

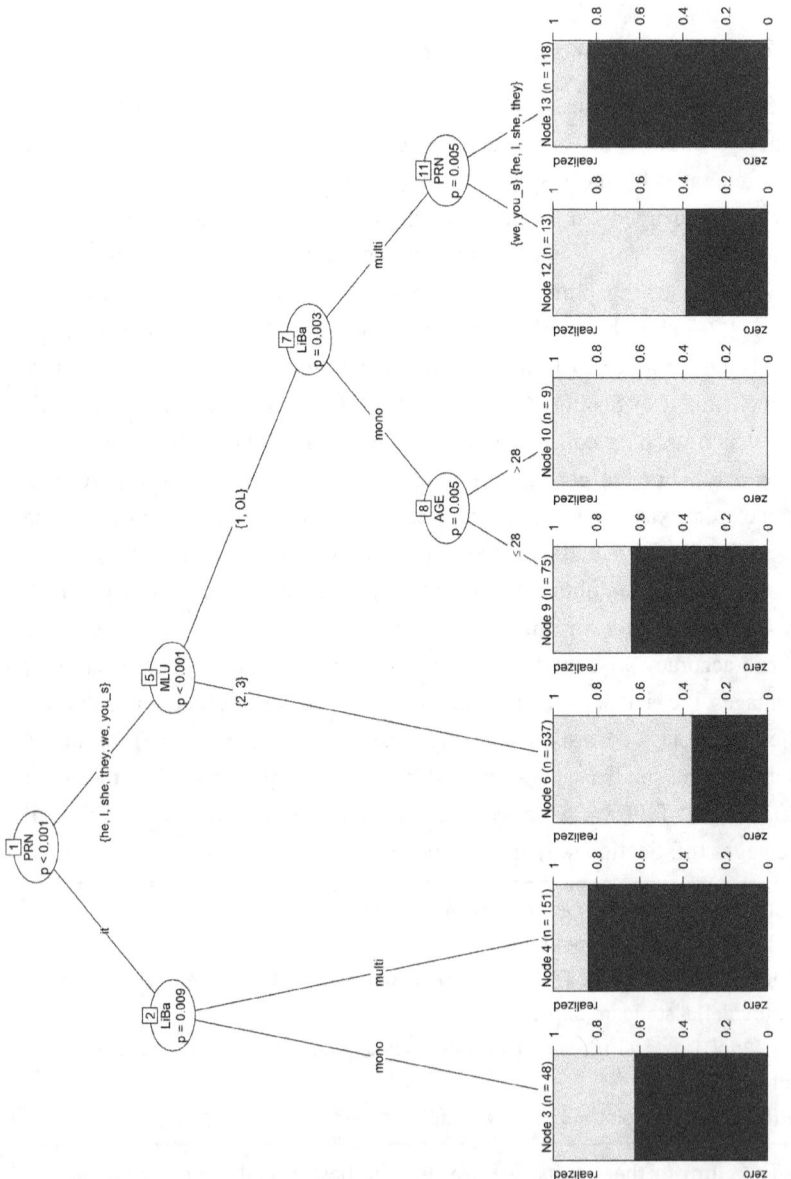

Figure 5 *Subpro* data: PrInDT result.

despite our restrictions in ctestv on which ethnicities of children and which MLU groups could cluster in a split. Therefore, we did not find any indication for questioning, let alone rejecting, our prior theoretical assumptions and thus expectations, which had led to the restrictions. However, this part of the method helped us eliminate trees that would have been contradictory to the vast majority of trees (944 out of 999 repetitions) and thus difficult, if not impossible, to interpret.

The tree in Figure 5 – and all following decision trees – are not explained in every detail (i.e., by commenting on every split). Instead, we focus on the prediction rules and the realization of the variable in the root split, while also providing a general summary of the most important findings. For constructing the prediction rules, we apply the default method that the class with the higher frequency is predicted in a terminal node. The **PrInDT** function also offers the possibility to alter this default setting by defining an alternative minimum frequency for the prediction of the smaller class other than 0.5 (cf. help(PrInDT)). For example, if the threshold is set to 0.6, the smaller class is only chosen if its frequency in a terminal node is higher than 0.6; otherwise the larger class is chosen.

As Figure 5 shows, *zero* is predicted if the subject pronoun (PRN) is *it* (Node 1) for both monolingual and multilingual children (Nodes 3 and 4). Alternatively, if the subject pronoun is not *it*, *zero* is predicted for monolingual children younger than 28 months and MLU=1 or OL[3] (Node 9), or if the subject pronoun is not *it*, *we*, or *you_s* (you singular) and the child belongs to MLU group 1 or OL and has a multilingual background (Node 13). In all other nodes (6, 10, 12), *realized* is predicted.

The model has revealed that the intralinguistic predictor "pronoun type" has the strongest impact on the realization of subject pronouns (Nodes 1, 11). *Zero* pronouns most prominently occur for the pronoun *it*; this means either semantically empty dummy *it* (expletive it; "It is raining") or referential *it* ("My cat, it is black"). The reasons why the most significant difference (Node 1) is found for pronoun type *it* is most likely intralinguistic in nature. It comes as no surprise that the rate of *zero* subject-pronoun realization is high for the semantically empty dummy *it* (expletive *it*), since these forms have no semantic referent. What is interesting, though, is that the two other types of *it*, and in particular referential *it*, behave similarly to expletive *it*, even though they have a clear semantic referent. The similarities in behavior must therefore be due to the phonological similarities between the three types (cf. Buschfeld 2020: 182) and

---

[3] OL is a group of four outlier children that strongly diverge from the other children regarding their age in relation to the syntactic complexity of their utterances. These have therefore been excluded from their age groups to not skew the results.

phonological assimilation/elision in forms such as *it*'s, which are frequent in spoken discourse.

For the remaining pronoun types (*I*, *you_s*, *he*, *she*, *we*, *they*), an age-related effect can be seen in Nodes 5 and 8 on the right side of the tree as MLU relates to age (cf. Section 2.1.1). For older children (MLU=2 or 3; Node 6), monolingual children older than 28 months (Node 10), and multilingual children for the pronouns *we* and *you_s* (Node 12), *realized* is predicted. In the two latter cases, though, only small numbers of tokens exist (9 in Node 10, 13 in Node 12), so these results need to be taken with a grain of salt.

In a next step, we applied the functions **RePrInDT** and **OptPrInDT** to our data to further improve the **PrInDT** analysis. By means of **RePrInDT**, accuracies of different combinations of percentages of the large and small classes can be compared to identify the combination of percentages leading to the highest accuracy of the model. However, our additional application did not lead to an improvement of balanced accuracy (cf. Weihs & Buschfeld 2021c for further discussion).

In the call of **OptPrInDT**, we need to specify the maximal percentages psmax and plmax to be applied to the small and the large classes, respectively, and the distances dists and distl to the next lower percentage for the small and the large classes that should be applied. We used the defaults plmax=0.09, dists=0.1, and distl=0.01 and the re-specification psmax=0.95. Thus the two largest percentages tested for the small class are 0.95 and 0.85. Based on these specifications, an automatic optimization procedure identifies the best combination of percentages and the corresponding tree. We use the following R-code:

```
# datazero,"real",ctestv as for PrInDT
outOpt <- OptPrInDT(datazero,"real",ctestv,N=799,psmax=0.95,conf.level=0.99)
outOpt
plot(outOpt$tree1st)
```

The **OptPrInDT** analysis has returned the tree in Figure 6 as the best tree generated by the procedure. This tree is based on 7.5% of the large and 90% of the small class. The balanced accuracy of this tree is 0.7047, which is only slightly better than 0.7033 for the tree in Figure 6, but some interesting differences exist between the trees.

In Figure 6, *zero* is predicted if the pronoun is *it* and ethnicity is Singaporean Chinese or Indian (Node 6), or if the pronoun is *it* and ethnicity is English ancestral, English mixed, or migrant, or Singaporean mixed and the children are younger than 67 months (Node 4). *Zero* is further predicted if the pronoun is not *it*, *we*, or *you_s*; MLU is 1 or OL; and the linguistic background is *multi*

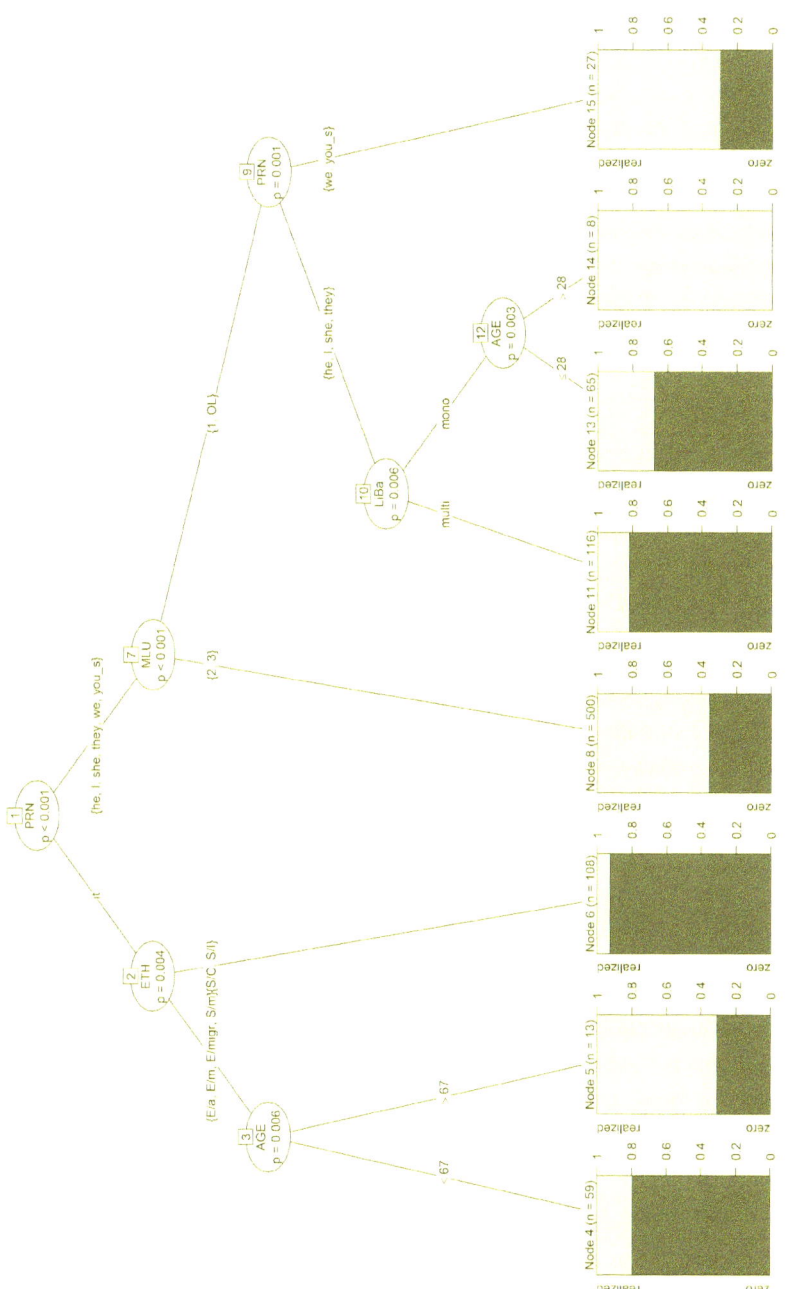

Figure 6 *Subpro* data: OptPrInDT result.

(Node 11) or the child is very young (AGE ≤ 28 months; Node 13). In all other instances, *realized* is predicted (Nodes 5, 8, 14, 15).

Therefore, the two trees in Figures 5 and 6 are very similar. However, ethnicity is part of the optimized tree in Figure 6 and splits the children mainly into those growing up in Singapore and those growing up in England. The one child of mixed ethnic origin from Singapore that clusters with the English children has a Malaysian mother and a Turkish father and thus a different acquisitional background. The general differentiation between English and Singaporean children adds a strong result to the analysis, which confirms our earlier expectations on how the differences in the input the children receive (i.e., traditional native English input versus SingE input) must have an influence on language acquisition. Furthermore, the comparison of trees confirms our earlier claim that trying out different methods, generating more than one tree, and comparing their results may yield more detailed and flexible results, which, as long as they do not contradict each other (but see our suggestion on how to avoid uninterpretable results in Section 4.2), clearly enhance our understanding of the data and overall linguistic situation.

5.1.2 Modeling by Structured Subsampling

In Section 5.1.1, we used random subsampling of the tokens/observations for undersampling. This means that for the sample utilized for estimating the best tree, tokens are randomly eliminated from all children. **PrInDTCstruc** was created to identify those children that are most representative for the complete group of children by first sampling from a natural substructure of the data, in this example from the children for which subject-pronoun realizations were observed. Representativeness is achieved by identifying the subgroup of children that leads to the highest accuracy of the model. For the children chosen by this first subsampling procedure, additional undersampling can be applied to balance the tokens of the two classes. Moreover, we also allow for subsampling from the predictors (i.e., we can impose a restriction on the number of predictors the model is built from). This way, features are excluded from model building in the corresponding repetitions of subsampling. This leads to larger variation in the resulting models and is thus methodologically similar to bagging or random forests (cf. Section 4.3).

For an application of **PrInDTCstruc**, we first have to specify the details of structured subsampling. These specifications are summarized in a list called Struc:

```
Struc <- list(name=CHILDzero,check="datazero$ETH",labs=labs)
```

name(=CHILDzero) is the name of the variable representing the substructure. In this variable, we distinguish two categories (Singaporean and English children; cf. Section 4.5.1). check(="datazero$ETH") is the name of the variable that contains the relevant information about the categories of the substructure. The values of check characterizing the categories are defined in the rows of the matrix labs (i.e., in labs[1,] and labs[2,] for the first and second categories, respectively). In these definitions, the R-function c(...) generates a list of the specified elements. The names of the categories are defined in rownames(labs). The respective R-code reads as follows:

```
# datazero,CHILDzero as for PrInDT
labs <- matrix(nrow=2,ncol=3) # definition of labs; 2 rows, 3 columns
labs[1,] <- c("S/C","S/I","S/m")
labs[2,] <- c("E/a","E/m","E/migr")
rownames(labs) <- c("Singaporean children","English children")
Struc <- list(name=CHILDzero,check="datazero$ETH",labs=labs)
```

We applied all versions of structured subsampling described in Section 4.5.1. Version d (vers="d"), which includes first subsampling from the children (with additional undersampling of the large class) and then from the predictors for each subsample of the children, turned out to deliver the highest accuracy. We used the defaults for the number of predictors (Pit=c(3,4,5,6)) and the number of elements of the substructure (Eit=c(17,18,19,20,21)). In the function **PrInDTCstruc**, these defaults are defined in dependence on the maximum number of predictors (P=7) and children per country (E=21) to be Pit = P-4, P-3, ..., P-1 and Eit = E-4, E-3, ..., E, respectively. After some testing, N=19 appeared to be sufficient for the number of repetitions of the selections of predictors and elements. Overall, this amounts to $5 \times 19 \times 4 \times 19 = 7{,}220$ repetitions since structured subsampling determines the best model over all combinations of the numbers of predictors (four different) and elements (five different). We employ the following R-code:

```
# datazero,"real",CHILDzero,ctestv as for PrInDT
# substructure Struc as above
outstruc <- PrInDTCstruc(datazero,"real",ctestv,Struc,vers="d", N=19,conf.level=0.99)
print(outstruc)
plot(outstruc) # standard plots
```

The print and plot statements are of the same kind for all PrInDT functions and are thus not shown in the following applications.

When we turn to the results, the best model from this call of **PrInDTCstruc** is illustrated in Figure 7. The model is based on twenty children from Singapore

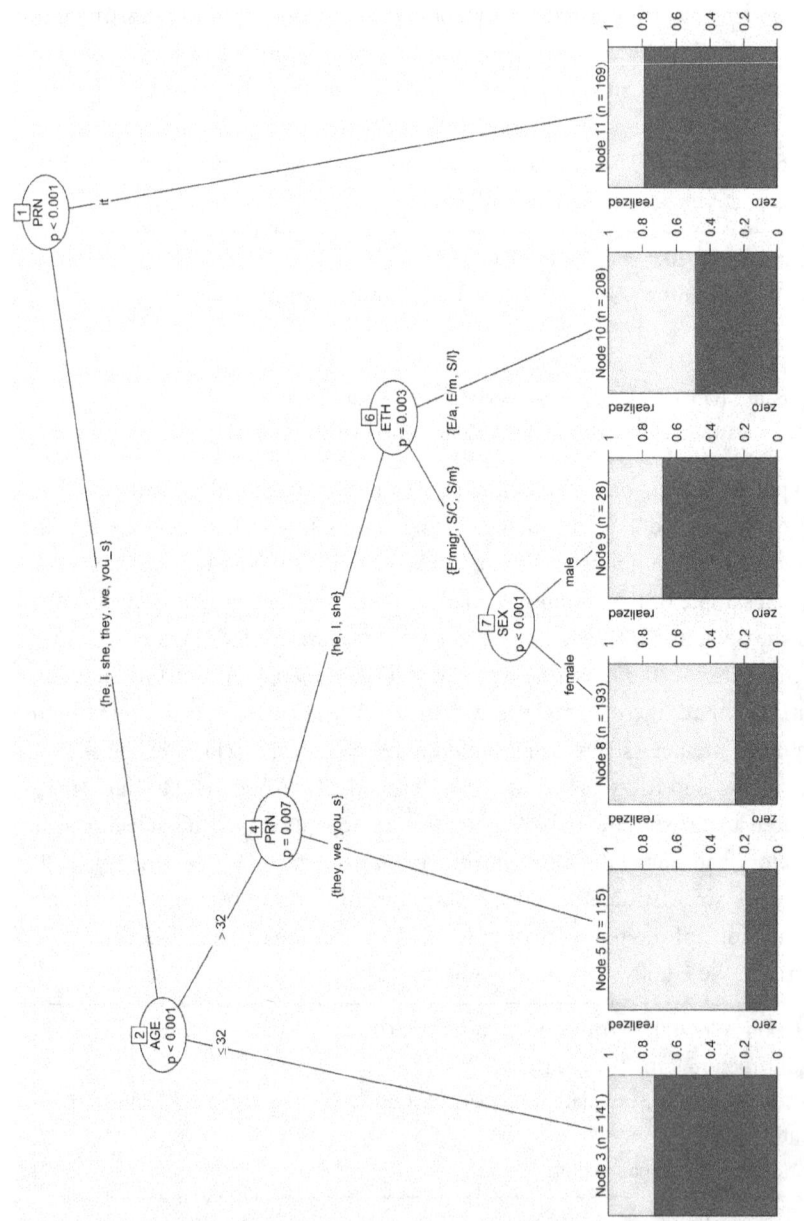

Figure 7 *Subpro* data: PrInDTCstruc result.

and England, respectively, and on the four predictors PRN, ETH, AGE, and SEX. This model, again, is a slight improvement to the trees presented in Figures 5 and 6, since its balanced accuracy amounts to 0.7059.

Again, the type of pronoun is the most important predictor, but age and ethnicity play important roles, too. For the first time, SEX has made it into the tree. This might be the result of the specific distribution and interplay of gender, age, and ethnicity in the data set or might, of course, show that female children have a stronger inclination toward realized subject pronouns (i.e., the traditional standard structure). This would be an interesting finding, generally in line with sociolinguistic theory, but we cannot discuss this in detail due to special restrictions and the mainly statistical focus of the Element at hand.

In the following, we turn to yet another application variant of PrInDT on the *subpro* data set to illustrate how our approach can be applied to a diverse set of linguistic data, meeting several data-related challenges that have been reported for variationist linguistic studies.

5.2 Subject-Pronoun Realization with Unbalanced Predictor: Nested Resampling

The data set *nessubpro*, which aims to analyze subject-pronoun realization with unbalanced predictors (cf. Section 2.1.2), is characterized not only by a high imbalance in the class variable "class" but also in one of the independent variables, namely SPEAKER. This variable we call nesting variable (=nesvar), since we employ the two-step procedure **NesPrInDT** for nested undersampling (cf. Section 4.5.2) to also level the imbalance between the two levels of SPEAKER, namely child and adult (cf. Section 2.1.2).

In the following, we mainly report the analytical steps and results of a study by Weihs and Buschfeld (2021b) to illustrate this procedure. As a first step of **NesPrInDT**, we randomly undersampled the adult data at repin=10 repetitions to match the size of the child corpus. Then, for each undersample of the adult data and the full sample of the child data, we randomly undersampled the large class to plarge=6% and used the full sample of the small class (psmall=1) at N=999 repetitions for a confidence level of conf.level=0.95. No interpretability restrictions apply (ctestv=NA). The R-code reads as follows:

```
# data = nessubpro data
nesvar <- "SPEAKER"
nesunder <- data$SPEAKER # data of nesvar
data[,nesvar] <- list(NULL) # nesvar not used as a predictor
outNes <- NesPrInDT(data,"class",ctestv=NA,N=999,plarge=0.06,psmall=1,
conf.level=0.95,nesvar=nesvar,nesunder=nesunder,repin=10)
```

Figure 8 illustrates the best tree generated by **NesPrInDT**, which has a balanced accuracy of 0.5741 on the full sample, which is, strictly speaking, far too low to yield reliable results. Nevertheless, we continue the analysis and interpretation for illustration of the approach, as it might yield higher results for other data sets. As Figure 8 shows, again, pronoun type is the most important predictor, followed by different splits of AGE, MLU, and ETH. Since the pronoun-type categorization is more fine-grained than for *subpro* (cf. Section 2.1.2), the tree shows more fine-grained splits, too. These, however, do not contradict any of the earlier results since the different types of *it*, again, cluster together and demonstrative *this* and *that* (both highly referential) are grouped with the referential pronouns.

Since this particular study aims to investigate whether quantitative differences exist between child and adult speakers in their use of *realized* and *zero* pronouns, we focus on those aspects of the tree related to this objective. As Node 2 illustrates, we find a general AGE-motivated split of the data between participants 145 months (12 years) or younger and those older than 145 months, with the younger participants showing a higher inclination toward *zero it* pronouns (all three types; cf. Section 5.1.1) than the older ones. This represents a significant difference between the child and adult participants, as the children are all 12 years or younger, while the adults are all older than 18.

For referential *I*, *you_s*, *he*, *she*, *we*, *they*, however, the Singaporean children in MLU-group 3 (children older than seven years and under formal language instruction in school) cluster with the adults from Singapore (Node 5). This does not necessarily contradict the general finding for pronoun types *it* but once again confirms that results might simply be different for different pronoun types. Alternatively, this finding might be interpreted as indicative of an early-stage age-grading effect. It has often been observed that children behave differently from adults, but that under increased formal pressure toward more standardized language use (e.g., through the school system), they may change toward more standardized adult speech forms.

For referential and demonstrative pronouns, MLU group 2 is further split by age at 66 months (5 years, 6 months; Node 13). At first sight, it is also surprising that the older children are the ones that realize *zero* pronouns significantly more frequently than the younger ones, since normally the younger children go through a zero-subject phase in language acquisition. However, this finding can be explained on the basis of the data set since the MLU group 2 children older than 66 months all speak Chinese and thus a null subject language as their other L1.

Furthermore, a rough review of the data indicated that the adults may be very heterogeneous in their pronoun realization. To analyze this, we decided to

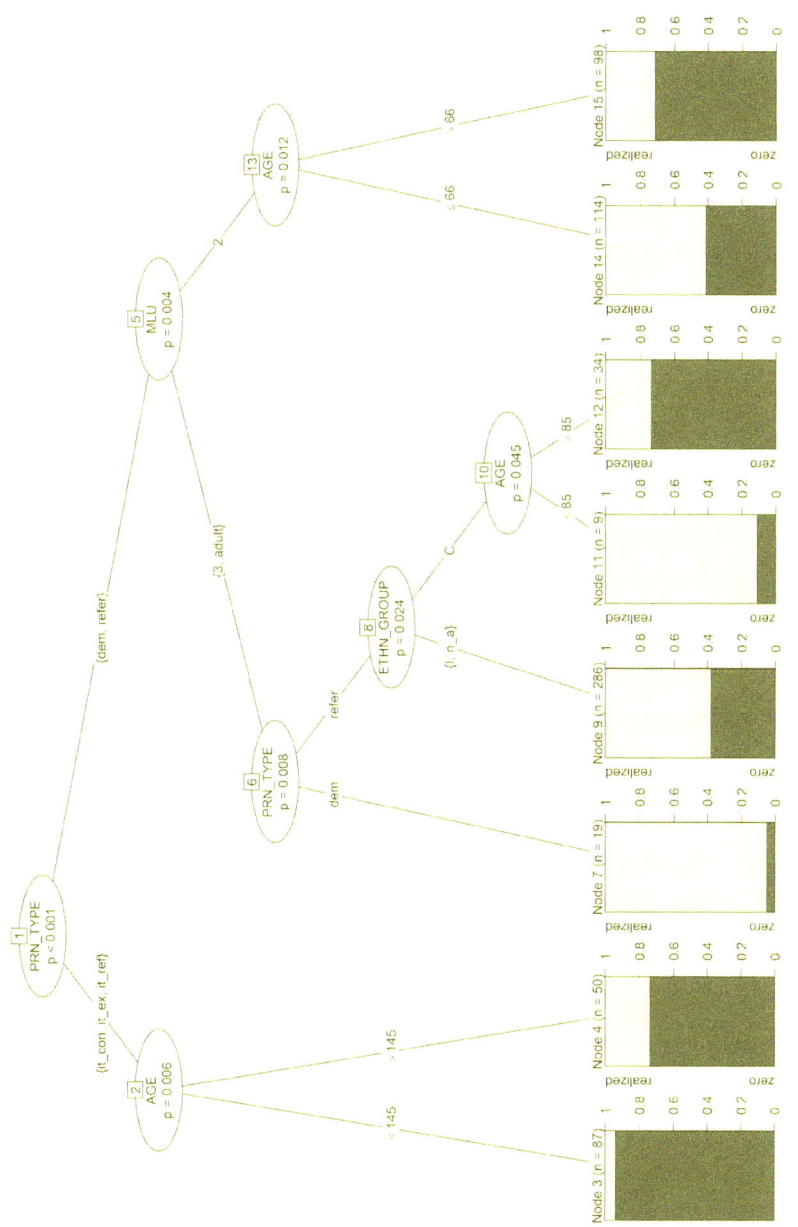

Figure 8 Subject pronouns in the child and adult corpora: NesPrInDT result.

analyze parts of the adult data individually and compare the results. Therefore, we decided to divide the adult data into eight parts according to their order of appearance in the data set (divt=8 in the following PrInDT-code) and used the function **PrInDTAllparts** to build trees on the divt parts of the adult data together with the complete child data.

```
# data,nesvar as for NesPrInDT
outParts <- PrInDTAllparts(data,"class",ctestv=NA,conf.level=0.99,nesvar=nesvar,divt=8)
```

The results show that the balanced accuracies of the eight trees that comprise all tokens of the children and one-eighth of the adult tokens show very different values: One tree has a balanced accuracy of 0.5, six trees of 0.566, and one tree of 0.805. In the model with the highest accuracy, the smaller class appeared much more often in the adult data than in the other parts. On the one hand, this improves the accuracy. On the other hand, this confirms the heterogeneity of the adults' sample. Unfortunately, no sociolinguistic information on the adults' exact age, ethnicity, social background, or gender is available, which might help explain the heterogeneity in the adult sample.

Not being able to account for this heterogeneity by means of sociolinguistic variables is, of course, problematic when it comes to discussing potential language change. Increasing numbers of L1 speakers of SingE have been reported since the 1980s (e.g., Kwan-Terry 1986). This suggests that change from L2 to L1 has already started in the adult population of the 1990s, and we do not know whether any of the speakers in the 1990s corpus are L1 speakers of English, which is another important piece of information the ICE-Singapore does not offer. In general, we cannot expect that the change we observe has taken place solely in the approximately 20 years between our two data sets. Therefore, the heterogeneity observed for the adult data set might be indicative of language change in progress, in which old (here more standard) structures might still be widely in use but gradually replaced by the more and more accepted nostandard ones, depending on the speakers' age and ethnic and sociolinguistic backgrounds.

In the following section (Section 5.3), we turn toward our next PrInDT application of three-class classification trees.

5.3 Past-Tense Marking: Three-Class Classification Trees

The *past* data set (cf. Section 2.1.3) is analyzed by means of the function **PrInDTMulev** (cf. Section 4.5.3), since the target variable has three categories, i.e., *marked*, *unmarked*, and *finish*. For this case, we apply the "one-versus-rest strategy" of classification (i.e., we investigate how individual categories [classes] differ from the joint set of other classes). This yields an individual model for each class. From these models, an estimate of the individual probability of each class is derived for each observation. Then, for each observation, the class with the highest probability is chosen as a prediction (cf. Section 4.5.3).

So far, the *past* data set was only analyzed based on the full sample by means of logistic regression and decision trees (Buschfeld 2020: 208–211) and by means of the PrInDT approach in Buschfeld and Weihs (2024), who modeled the class *marked* as the standard level against the nonstandard levels *unmarked* and *finish* as a joint class.

By means of **PrInDTMulev**, however, we analyzed the three classes as independent levels. For each of the one-versus-rest two-class classifications, the percentages to balance classes are chosen automatically so that the larger class is subsampled to the size of the smaller class. For the **PrInDTMulev** analysis, we used the following R-code:

```
# data in datapast, target in "class", ctestv as for datazero
outpast <- PrInDTMulev(datapast,"class",ctestv,N=999,conf.level=0.99)
```

As illustrated in Figure 9, when predicting *finish* versus the two other classes, the most important predictor is LiBa, which splits the children between *bili1* and *multi2* children, on the one hand, and the rest of the children (i.e., *bili2*, *mono*, *mono+*, and *multi1*), on the other. The categories *bili1* and *multi2* include children who started to acquire two languages before the age of two. Obviously, this property leads to a 100% usage of *finish* as a past marking for all verbs not belonging to the nine most frequent ones (cf. Section 2.1.3).

This finding is not necessarily contradictory, though it needs to be taken with a grain of salt and cannot be overgeneralized since the other bilingual and multilingual acquisitional background types that are grouped together with the monolingual children in the tree also contain children who started to acquire two or more languages before the age of two. The reason behind this may simply be that the bi- and multilingual children do not all behave the same. In particular in the Singaporean cohort, we find huge differences between the children, especially with respect to the use of *finish*. Firstly, this form is not frequently used; secondly, it is distributed across only a handful of children and therefore seems to constitute a special form, which has (not yet?) found wide societal distribution.

The best trees for the classes *unmarked* versus rest and *marked* versus rest are very complex and not further discussed here. The balanced accuracies of the individual trees are 0.7857, 0.7784, and 0.8312 for *marked*, *unmarked*, and *finish*, respectively. All three trees are combined for the prediction of the true

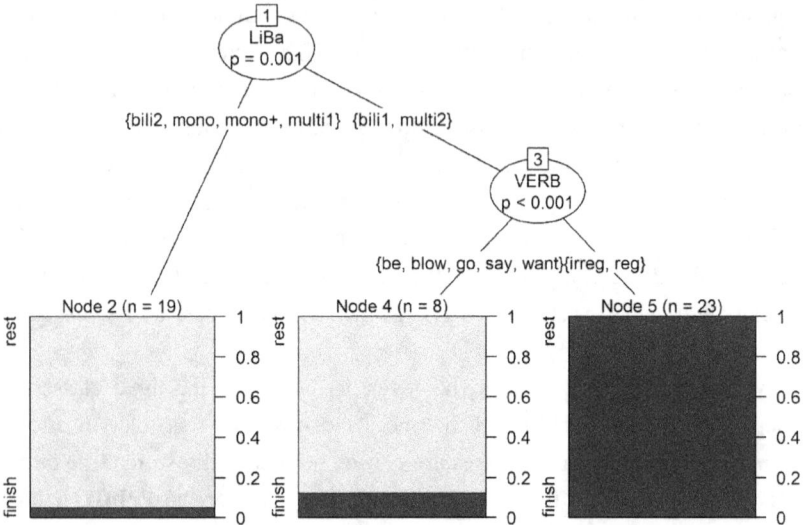

Figure 9 Best tree for the class *finish* versus the other two classes: PrInDTMulev result.

class of each observation in the following way: From the individual trees, an estimate of the probability of each class is derived for each observation. The class with the highest probability is chosen as the prediction (cf. Section 4.5.3 and the beginning of this section). This leads to a balanced accuracy of the combined models of 0.678, which is quite reasonable.

We consider the confusion matrix introduced in Section 3.2.4.2 for a detailed comparison of the observed classes and their predictions. The matrix appears as follows:

prediction	finish	marked	unmarked
finish	23	327	288
marked	0	1033	93
unmarked	2	285	362

This shows that taking into account all three classes, the category *finish* is nearly perfectly predicted (cf. column "finish") since only 2 of the 25 past realizations of the class *finish* are misclassified (to the category *unmarked*). For the other categories, only 63% of *marked* and 49% of *unmarked* are correctly predicted.

5.4 Vowel-Length Realization: Regression Trees

In a next step, we turn to the last of the Singapore data sets (i.e., the *vowel* data set), described in Section 2.1.4. This data set was also already analyzed in

Buschfeld (2020: 251), and first results were introduced in Section 3.2.3.1 to illustrate the general functionality of linear regression. In Section 5.4.1, we present the results from a first PrInDT analysis by means of **PrInDTreg**. In Section 5.4.2, we compare the results from the linear regression model to our PrInDT results.

5.4.1 Modeling by Random Subsampling

For the analysis by means of **PrInDTreg** (cf. Section 4.5.4), we employ the default percentages pobs=c(0.90,0.70) and ppre=c(0.90,0.70) to subsample the observations and predictors, respectively. The R-code reads as follows:

```
# data in datavowel, target in "vowel_length", ctestv as for subpro
outreg <- PrInDTreg(datavowel,"vowel_length",ctestv,N=999,conf.level=0.99)
```

When it comes to the results, the best tree (cf. Figure 10) identifies lexeme as the most relevant predictor. The model has an R^2 of 0.5117, which is rather low. However, which accuracies are acceptable for model construction, in particular for phonological analyses that are often characterized by strong inter- and intraspeaker variability, has, to our best knowledge, not yet been conclusively discussed (cf. Section 3.2.5).

The interpretation of a regression tree is more complicated than of a classification tree since the mean of all observations in a terminal node is used as the prediction for this terminal node. We restrict ourselves to just elaborating on outstanding findings. For long vowels as in the words *bee*, *cheese*, *key*, or *sea*, the prediction is much higher than the mean of vowel lengths for all vowels (of 199.3 ms; cf. Section 3.2.1). This is most prominently the case if vowel_maximum_pitch is high and vowel_minimum_pitch is low (Node 8). This finding can be interpreted in terms of the behavior of the children in the picture-naming task (cf. Section 2.1.4), as some of the children playfully but artificially lengthened the words at a very high pitch (e.g., This is a *beeeeeeeee*). On the other hand, the lowest vowel lengths are realized for shorter vowels, as in *chicken*, *fish*, *lip*, *print*, *scissor*, *stick*, and surprisingly *cheek* if speech rate is very low (Node 13) or if speech rate is not high and neither is vowel-maximum pitch (Node 15). The vowel length of *cheek* appears out of line since it normally belongs to the class of long vowels, but our results have revealed that the vowel in *cheek* is one of those vowels that the children pronounced particularly short (i.e., with a mean vowel length of *cheek* of 147.1 ms versus the overall mean vowel length of 199.3 ms). Furthermore, the lexemes *pig* and *ship* are grouped together with the longer vowels in Node 1, though their mean lengths are only slightly larger than the mean (cf. the result in Section 5.4.3).

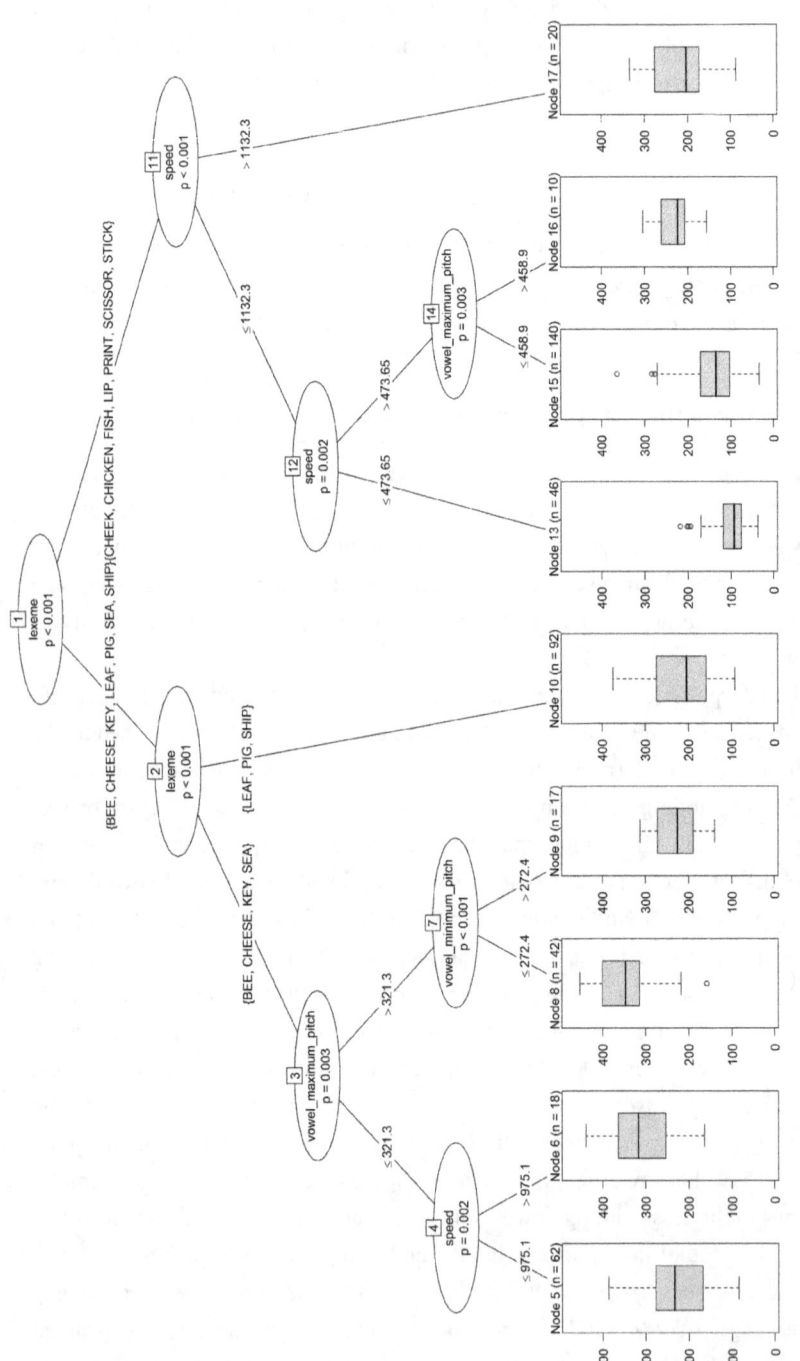

Figure 10 Vowel length: PrInDTreg result.

5.4.2 Comparison with Linear Regression

We will now compare the results of **PrInDTreg** and linear mixed-effects regression, as presented in Section 3.2.4, by means of two criteria (i.e., complexity of the model and its quality measured by R^2; cf. Section 4.1). The tree generated by **PrInDTreg** (cf. Figure 10) has 17 nodes, 4 influential predictors, and an R^2 of 0.5117. The model generated by linear mixed-effects regression has 12 coefficients of fixed-effect factors, 14 estimated individual increments for the lexemes, and an R^2 of 0.6068. Even though the linear mixed-effects regression model thus comes with a better accuracy, it has to be noted here that the quality of the models is not directly comparable since we used a significance level of 1% for the tree. With a maximum significance level of 5% or rather 10%, **PrInDTreg** gets larger trees with 21 or 25 nodes and higher R^2s of 0.5264 or 0.5482, respectively, which are still lower than the R^2 of the corresponding linear mixed-effects model. However, the R^2s of **PrInDTreg** measure not only the model fit on the training set, as the R^2 of the linear model, but also partly the predictive power on the test set (see Section 4.1); this comes at the expense of accuracy. Moreover, as already mentioned in Section 3.4.2, the models from linear mixed-effects regression and from **PrInDTreg** have quite a different structure and thus give very different insights. The mixed-effects model estimates main effects only, while our PrInDT model mainly estimates interactions. For example, the **PrInDTreg** tree illustrates the influence of vowel_minimum_pitch as restricted to higher values of vowel_maximum_pitch (Node 3 in Figure 10). Therefore, we think that our PrInDT model offers very valuable, additional information about the dependency of vowel_length on the other observed variables. Therefore, the models should not be considered competing approaches but complementary ones, each offering their own valuable insights.

Additionally, we compare the MuPDAR performance of linear models and trees for modeling of vowel_length, comparing the behavior of English (= Reference Speakers) and Singaporean children (= Target Speakers) (cf. Section 3.2.7). We distinguish four kinds of models:

- lmerTest: Model identified by the functions lmer and step (significance at 5% level) from the package lmerTest (cf. Section 3.2.4.1)
- lm: Fixed-effects linear model with the same fixed effects as in lmerTest plus lexeme, which was included as a stochastic effect in lmerTest
- ctree: Standard regression ctree
- optctree: Optimized ctree by **PrInDTreg** with default percentages

In the following, we will report the R^2s of steps (i) and (iv) of MuPDAR for the four different model types. For lmerTest, we report the R^2, including the stochastic effect.

R^2	lmerTest	lm	ctree	optctree
step (i)	0.67	0.63	0.56	0.60
step (iv)	0.47	0.30	0.19	0.29

Obviously, the accuracy of lm and optctree are comparable. Overall, the R^2s are much lower in step (iv) than in step (i). Figure 11 shows the step (iv) model for optctree.

Figure 11 indicates negative residuals for the lexemes {*cheek, cheese, lip, sea, stick*}. This means that Singaporean children have a tendency to shorten the vowels in these lexemes compared to children in England (observed value smaller than prediction by reference model), at least when word duration is not high (≤1038 ms). For the other lexemes and higher word durations (>1132.3 ms), vowel lengths are elongated for KIT-lexemes and shortened for FLEECE-lexemes. Obviously, the step (iv) models cannot fully explain the residuals because of the overall small R^2s.

5.4.3 Modeling by Structured Subsampling

Up to now, we have used random subsampling to identify the optimal tree. As for the classification analyses, we will apply structured subsampling for regression to identify the most representative children and predictors for this example in a next step. We employed all versions of subsampling presented in Section 4.5.1. Version d (vers="d") turned out to produce the best accuracy on the full sample. This means that accuracy was best when first performing subsampling from the elements of the substructure Struc (see Section 5.1.2 for a definition) and then subsampling from the predictors.

For version d of structured subsampling, the user has to choose the number of elements of the substructure (i.e., the number of children), as well as the number of predictors used for model construction. The overall data set contains 21 potential predictors and 22 children from Singapore, as well as 21 children from England. We tried to take a few children less for model building by only selecting 18, 19, 20, or 21 children for the two countries Singapore and England each (Mit=c(18,19,20,21)) and 100% or 70% of the predictors (ppre=c(1,0.7)). Moreover, some testing has revealed that it is advantageous for R^2 not to include all tokens of the chosen children. We chose either 95% or 70% of them (pobs=c(0.95,0.7)). To keep the number of repetitions acceptable, we only tried small numbers of repetitions M per number of children in Mit and N per percentage of predictors in ppre. Finally, we used M=10 and N=99 (default). Overall, we thus compared 10 × 4 × 2 × 2 × 99 = 15,840 models. The resulting R-code reads as follows:

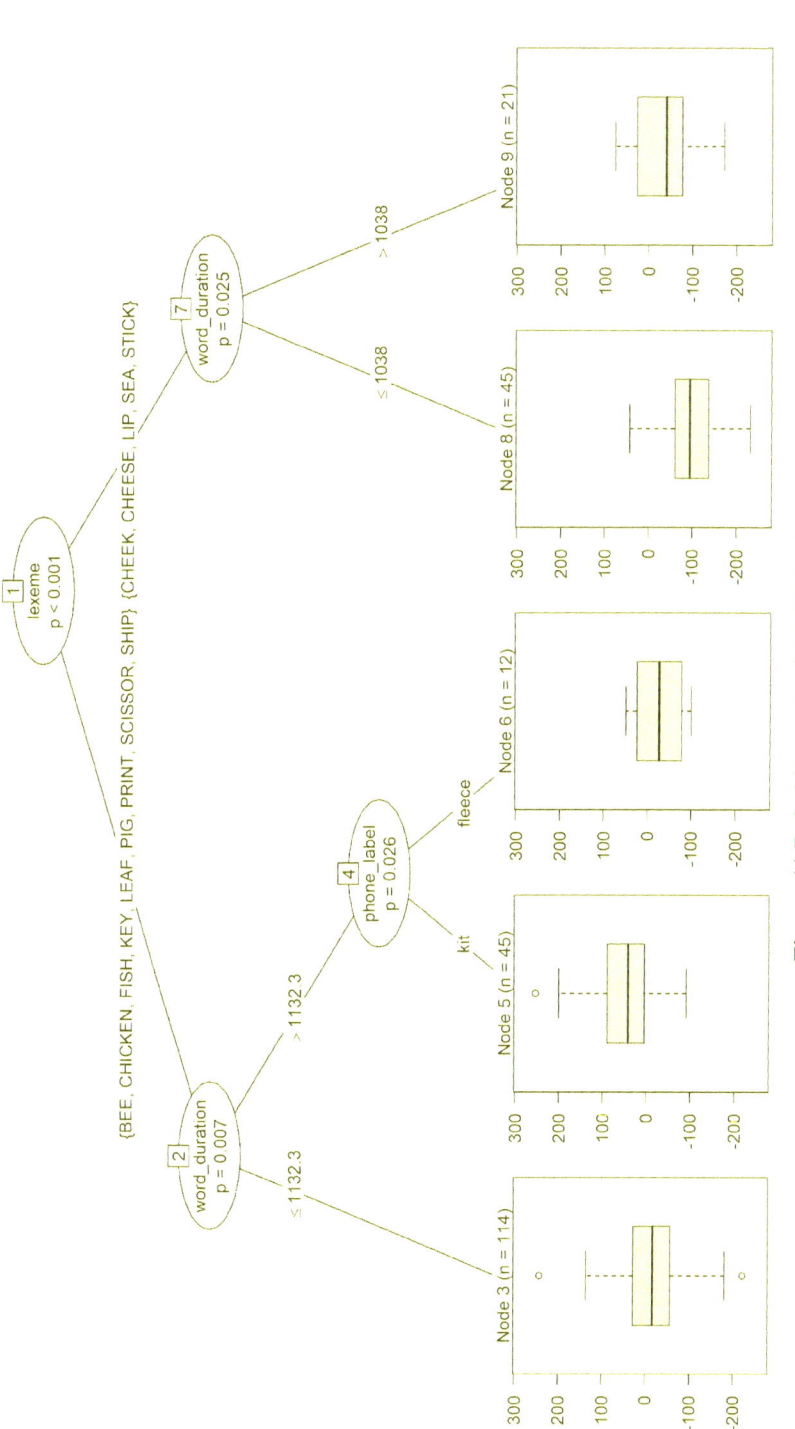

Figure 11 PrInDTreg tree for MuPDAR.

```
# data in datavowel, target in vowel_length, ctestv as for datazero
# Struc similar as for PrInDTCstruc:
Struc <- list(name=CHILDvowel,check="datavowel$ETH",labs=labs)
outregstruc <- PrInDTRstruc(datavowel,"vowel_length",ctestv,Struc,M=10,
Mit=c(18,19,20,21),pobs=c(0.95,0.7),ppre=c(1,0.7),vers="d",conf.level=0.99)
```

A comparison of the R^2s of all models has revealed that the best model is generated by means of 21 children from each of the two countries (i.e., only one Singaporean child is not included) and by leaving out 5% of the observations of the selected children randomly. The model with the best R^2 on the full sample is shown in Figure 12. Remarkably, by **PrInDTRstruc** the R^2 on the full sample was improved from 0.3933 (for the model based on the full data set) by 31% to 0.5158. This R^2 is even larger than the R^2 of 0.5117 for the best tree found by **PrInDTreg** with fully random selection of observations (cf. Figure 10).

When compared to the **PrInDTreg** tree in Figure 10, the predictors cons_class_l and cons_class_r have a significant impact on the model in Figure 12. Node 7, for example, shows that for long vowels (*bee, cheese, key, leaf, sea*) with small minimum pitch (≤ 270 Hz), vowel lengths differ for different kinds of consonants to their left. Furthermore, the lexemes *pig* and *ship* now cluster with the other lexemes with shorter vowels in the first split.

5.5 Landscaping Analysis: Multilabel Classification

For the *land* data set introduced in Section 2.2, the following analysis by means of the **PrInDTMulab** function (cf. Section 4.5.5) mainly reports and discusses the results in Buschfeld, Weihs, and Ronan (2024).

As presented in Section 4.5.5, at stage 1 **PrInDTMulab** models the endogenous variables individually based on the exogenous variables only (BR, Binary Relation). At stage 2, **PrInDTMulab** models the endogenous variables in dependence on the exogenous variables and additionally on the other endogenous variables (DBR, Dependent Binary Relation) and then inserts the BR predictions of the endogenous variables into the stage 2 model instead of the truly observed values (DBRT = DBR with true predictions).

For an application of **PrInDTMulab**, we first identify which variables of our data set are the dependent variables. The R-code names(dataland) shows the positions of the available variables in the data frame dataland. The positions of the dependent variables are identified and combined in the list inddep. In our example, the dependent variables French, Dutch, and English appear in the positions 9, 10, and 11 in dataland (inddep <- c(9:11)). The positions of the most important independent variables selected for stage 1 can be specified in the list

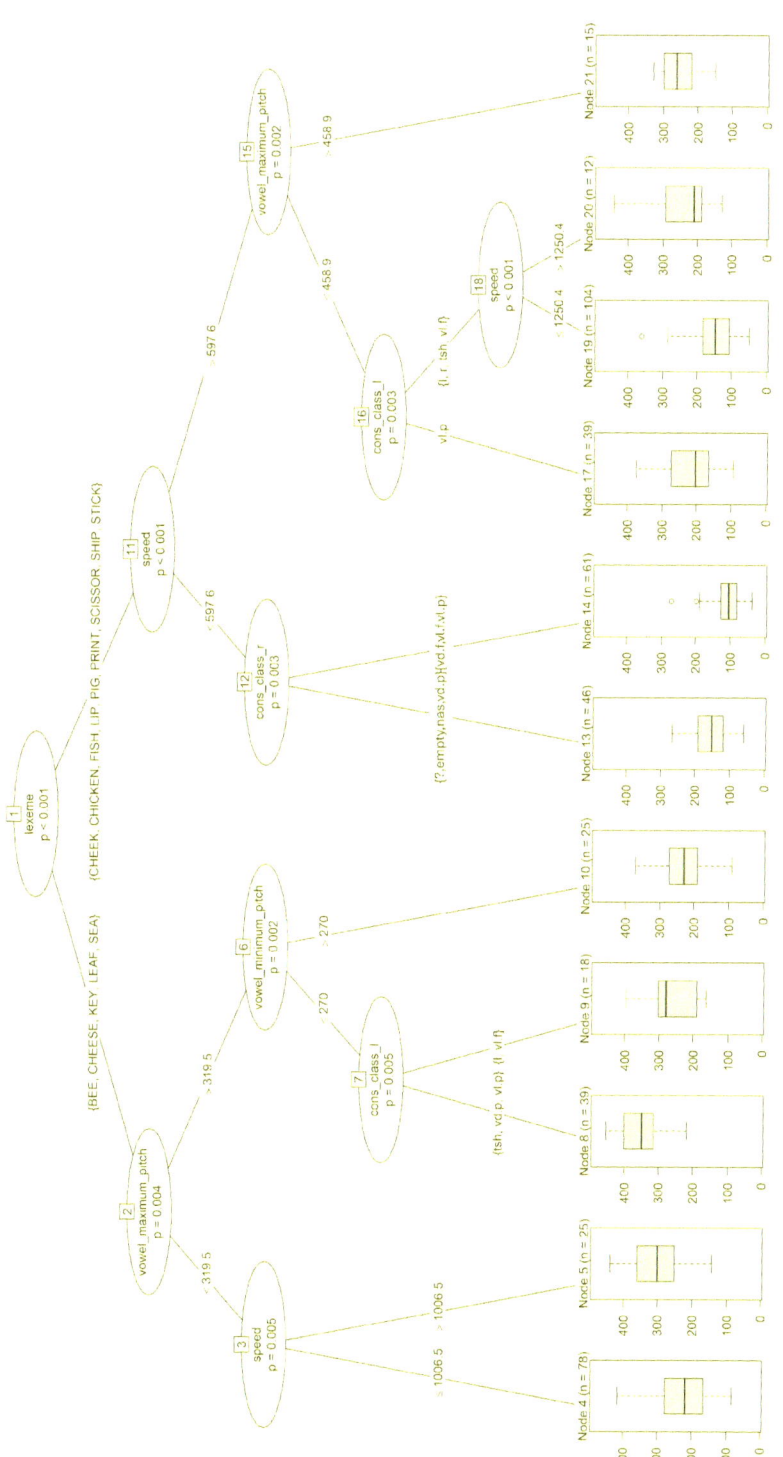

Figure 12 Vowel length: PrInDTRstruc result.

indind. At stage 2, **PrInDTMulab** uses all independent variables (i.e., also some additional variables not used at stage 1 since their positions were not included in the list indind). In our analysis, the languages Italian, Spanish, and German, as well as the variable bn.unclear (cf. Table 4), are only considered as additional predictors for stage 2, since we wanted to first model the dependence on sign characteristics and only then the dependence on further languages. If indind is not specified, all independent variables are automatically used for stage 1, as well.

Furthermore, the subsampling percentages of the large and the small classes have to be specified for the different dependent variables French, Dutch, and English. These classes are defined as "language on the sign" and "language not on the sign." For the languages French and Dutch, "language on the sign" is the smaller class, considering all observed signs in the data set. This is particularly pronounced for Dutch, which only appears on 7.9% of the signs. English appears on 75% of the signs. The lists percl (for the large class) and percs (for the small class) include one percentage each per dependent class variable in the order of appearance in inddep. These percentages should help balance the classes. In our example, the difference between the percentages has to be large only for the language Dutch (second place) since Dutch appears much more seldom than the other languages. In contrast to most other analyses, we set the maximum significance level in the trees to 5% (instead of 1%). The R-code reads as follows:

```
names(dataland)
inddep <- c(9:11)
indind <- c(1:8,16)
outmult <- PrInDTMulab(dataland,ctestv=NA,indind=indind,inddep=inddep,
N=1001,percl=c(0.45,0.05,0.25),percs=c(0.75,0.95,0.75),conf.level=0.95)
```

Figure 13 illustrates the model for the prediction of English, without including the other languages as predictors.

It shows that the most important predictor for the use of English is the number of languages (Node 1). English is predicted to be on the sign (English present, indicated in light gray) if the number of languages on the sign is larger than 1 (Node 2). In Philipsburg, English is also predicted for monolingual signs that include one of the following: a proper noun in the form of a brand name in combination with further linguistic material (*bn+*), a company name, both on its own or with further linguistic material (*cn* or *cn+*), or just regular text that does not include a proper noun (*no*) (Node 5). Additionally, in Marigot English is predicted for monolingual signs of the types door sign or graffiti (Node 9). For all other combinations of predictors, English is predicted to be not present on the sign. This model has a balanced accuracy of 0.87 and is, therefore, quite reliable.

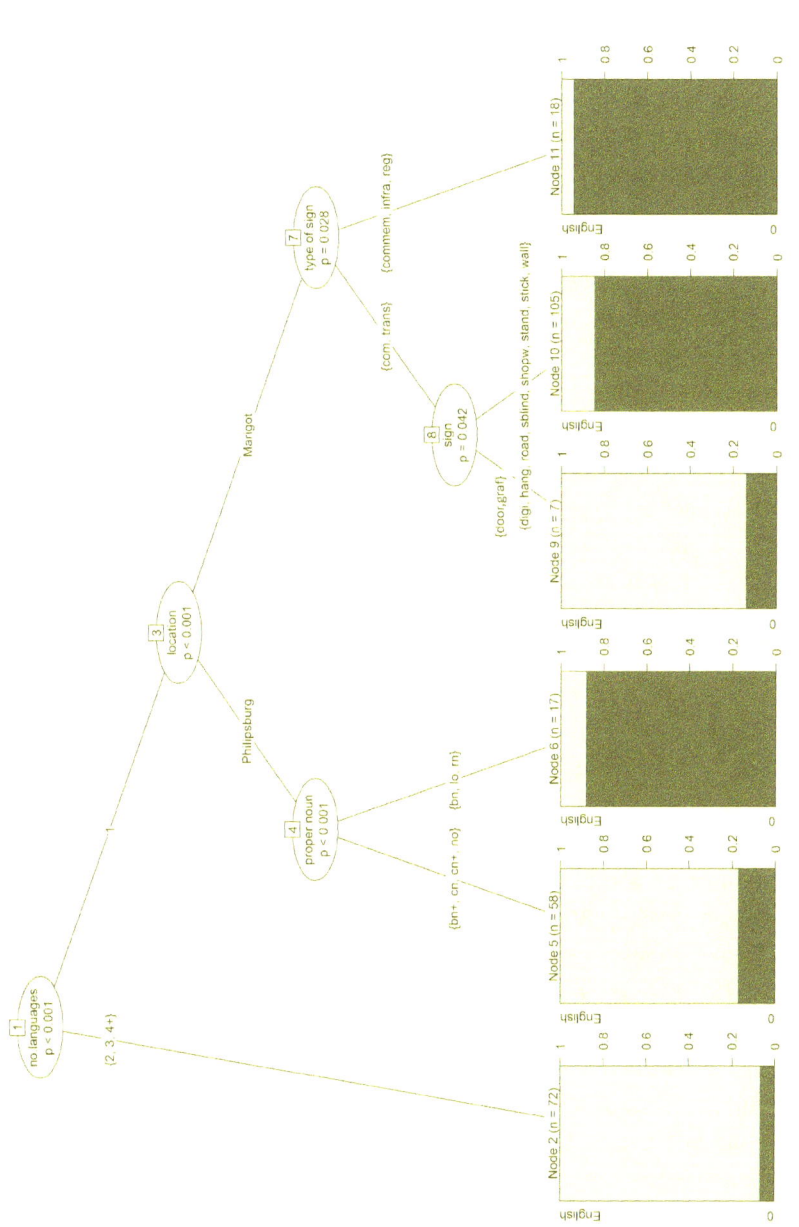

Figure 13 Prediction of English (without other languages as predictors, slightly adapted from Buschfeld et al. 2024: 322).

Figure 14 illustrates the prediction of English, including the other languages as predictors. For this model, the balanced accuracy is even higher (= 0.96). This does not come as a surprise, as the model can draw on additional predictors related to the languages on the sign. Again, the most important predictor is "number of languages" and English is predicted to be on the sign if the sign includes more than one language (Node 11). If only one language is displayed on a sign and this language is neither French nor Dutch and the language of a brandname is clear (admittedly a no-brainer at this point), and if no proper noun or proper nouns of the types brand name+, company name and company name+, or restaurant name+ are included, English is also predicted (Node 7). For all other contexts and combinations of predictors, English is predicted to not be part of the sign.

Because of space restrictions, we do not report the models for French and Dutch here (cf. Buschfeld, Weihs, & Ronan 2024 for further details). For some results for French, see our application and discussion of simultaneous classification models in Section 5.6.1.

To compare the accuracies of the individual models, Table 7 illustrates the balanced accuracies of the best individual trees. In general, the accuracies are highest for English, and as discussed earlier in this section, accuracies are always higher for the models including the other languages as predictors. However, for DBRT, the accuracies are lower again. In general, we have observed quite high balanced accuracies overall, in particular for a linguistic study, for which data sets are often characterized by strong inter- and even intraspeaker variability, which leads to lower predictability of the observed variables.

To also assess the quality of the findings of the multilabel analysis, we present the multilabel performance measures introduced in Section 4.5.5, as well as the mean balanced accuracy over all three labels. As Table 8 illustrates, performance measures are considerably lower for the multilabel analysis than for the monolabel analyses if all labels have to be predicted correctly (01-accuracy). However, the values of the 01-accuracy, and thus the predictive power for all predictions to be correct, are still high even though multilabel prediction is more complicated than single label prediction. Again, 01-accuracy is much higher for DBR than for BR but lower for DBRT. Therefore, it might well be that the improvements of the predictive power of the DBR model (0.8) over the BR model (0.65) are mainly caused by the rather unrealistic assumption that the labels are previously known when they should be predicted. This assumption is unnecessary for the DBRT approach, which works on the basis of true predictions from exogenous variables. In this case, the 01-accuracy goes down almost to the BR-value, namely to 0.69. The Hamming accuracy is similar to the mean balanced accuracy.

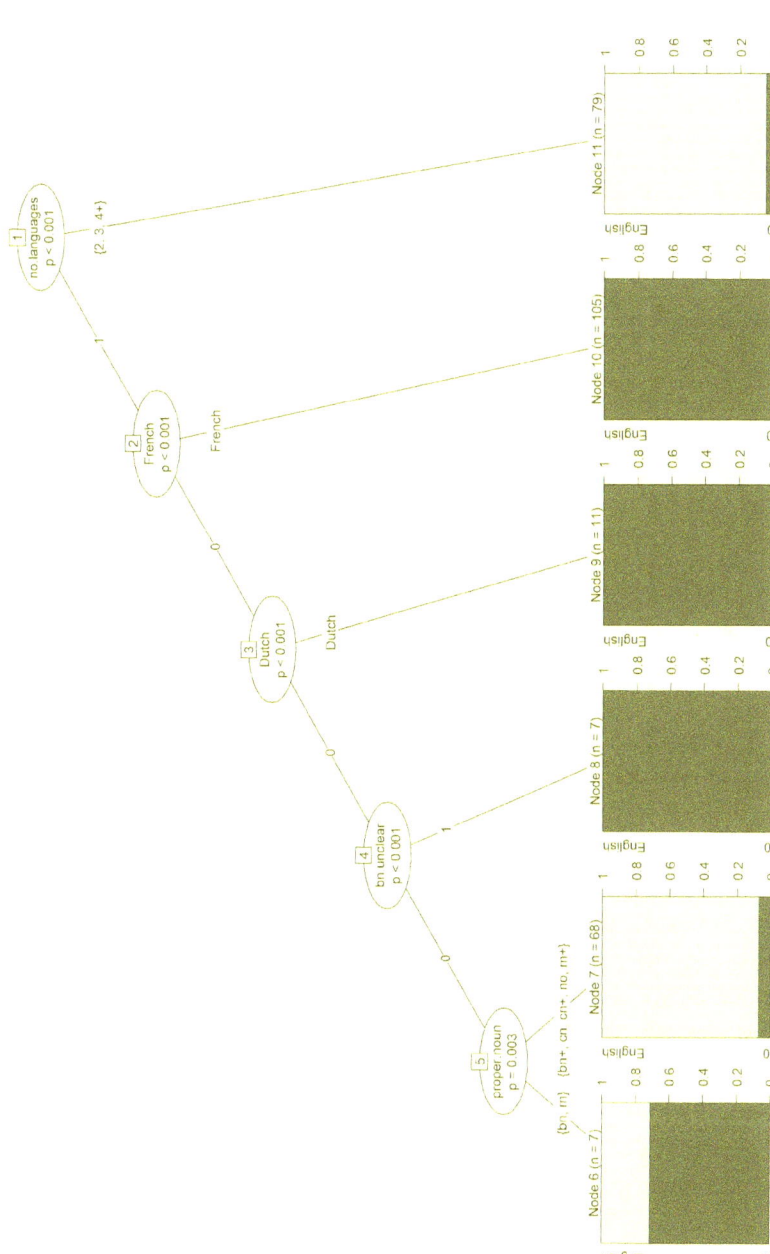

Figure 14 Prediction of English (with other languages as predictors; slightly adapted from Buschfeld et al. 2024: 323).

Table 7 Balanced accuracies of best individual trees
(adapted from Buschfeld et al. 2024: 326)

	Without languages BR	With languages DBR	With languages DBRT
English	0.87	0.96	0.86
French	0.82	0.92	0.83
Dutch	0.87	0.89	0.89

Table 8 Performance measures for multilabel analyses
(adapted from Buschfeld et al. 2024: 327)

	01-accuracy	Hamming accuracy	Mean balanced accuracy
without languages (BR)	0.65	0.84	0.85
with languages (DBR)	0.80	0.92	0.92
true predictions (DBRT)	0.69	0.84	0.86

5.6 Interdependent Models in Classification and Regression

In the final part of our application of PrInDT, we turn toward new methods for interdependent models, which are discussed in the following sections for the first time.

In interdependent models, two or more endogenous variables are modeled together and in dependence on each other and on potential exogenous predictors. We distinguish two approaches. Following Larsson et al. (2021), we distinguish cases where only the values of the exogenous variables are available to model the endogenous variables (*Exo-approach*) and cases where the values of the endogenous variables are directly available, and we can estimate models where the endogenous variables may also depend on each other (*Endo-approach*). In the *Exo-approach*, interdependency is limited to the usage of predictions of the endogenous variables as additional predictors from models based on the exogenous variables only. For values of the exogenous variables not used for model construction, such models can directly predict the endogenous variables. In the *Endo-approach*, models can be used, for instance, for unveiling relationships among the endogenous variables (cf. Section 4.5.6).

As described in Sections 4.5.1 and 4.5.4, both approaches consist of two stages. At stage 1 of the *Exo-approach*, we analyze the endogenous variables individually based on the exogenous variables only. At stage 2, we remodel the endogenous variables by including the predictions of the endogenous variables from stage 1 as additional predictors. At stage 1 of the *Endo-approach*, we base the model on the full sample and use the accuracy of this model as a benchmark for the stage 2 analysis. At stage 2, we try to improve the models from stage 1 by using structured subsampling. In the *EndoI-approach* (Endogenous Individual), we apply structured resampling independently to each endogenous variable. In the *EndoJ-approach* (Endogenous Joint), we look for the best models for the different endogenous variables by optimizing the mean accuracy over all endogenous variables based on the same set of elements and/or predictors for all endogenous variables. We refer to the results of the *Exo-approach* as REx (Results of *Exo-approach*) and to the results of the *Endo-approach* as REn (Results of *Endo-approach*).

5.6.1 Simultaneous Classification Models

As examples for simultaneous classification models, we apply **C2SPrInDT** and **SimCPrInDT** (two-stage classification by both the *Exo-*and *Endo-approache*s) to the *land* data set introduced in Section 2.2. This application aims to model whether the languages English, Dutch, and French (endogenous variables) are displayed on signs on the Caribbean island of St. Martin, in dependence of each other and of other characteristics of the signs like their location, their purpose, and so on (exogenous variables).

This data set was already analyzed by means of the function **PrInDTMulab** in Section 5.5 with a similar aim in mind. Stage 1 of **C2SPrInDT** equals stage 1 of **PrInDTMulab** (i.e., the outcomes are BR models). Stage 2 of **C2SPrInDT** is comparable with DBRT (i.e., stage 3 of **PrInDTMulab**), in which predictions of the endogenous variables are also employed as predictors. However, **C2SPrInDT** only needs the two stages introduced in Section 4.5.6.1 and finds an even better model for English (cf. Table 9).

As for **PrInDTMulab** (cf. Section 5.5), for both the *Exo-* and the *Endo-approaches*, we have to specify the feature numbers inddep of the endogenous variables. For **C2SPrInDT**, we use the same specifications as in **PrInDTMulab** and the following R-code:

```
# dataland,indind,inddep,N,percl,percs as for PrInDTMulab
out2SC <- C2SPrInDT(dataland,indind=indind,inddep=inddep,N=1001,
    percl=percl,percs=percs,conf.level=0.95)
```

For **SimCPrInDT** at stage 2 (*Endo-approach*), version b of structured subsampling is implemented (i.e., we only apply subsampling to the predictors; cf.

Table 9 Balanced accuracies (ba) of the language models in REx, REn, DBRT, and DBR

Stage	French	Dutch	English	Mean ba
REx1 = BR	0.8187992	0.8704353	0.8706221	0.8532855
DBRT	0.8268824	0.8852844	0.8610884	0.8577517
REx2	0.8268824	**0.8852844**	0.8653472	0.8591713
REn1	0.9211228	0.5995083	0.9402067	0.8202793
DBR	0.9162447	0.8852844	0.9620014	0.9211768
REnI	0.9299609	**0.9067920**	0.9620014	0.9329181
REnJ	0.9265670	**0.9067920**	0.9620014	0.9317868

Section 4.5.1). We repeatedly (M=12 times) used random (psize=)10 of the 13 exogenous variables and the endogenous variables as predictors. The results are directly comparable to the results of DBR in **PrInDTMulab** (cf. Section 5.5) since DBR uses all observed endogenous variables as additional predictors, too. Subsampling of the classes was also included with N=199 repetitions according to the lists percl, percs, introduced in Section 5.5. The R-code reads as follows:

```
# dataland,inddep,percl,percs as for PrInDTMulab
outSimC <- SimCPrInDT(dataland,inddep=inddep,
percl=percl,percs=percs,N=199,M=12,psize=10,conf.level=0.95)
```

In Table 9, the balanced accuracies for the languages French, Dutch, and English and the mean balanced accuracies are presented for **C2SPrInDT** (cf. rows REx1 and REx2) in comparison to BR and DBRT of **PrInDTMulab**. As we can see, the results of stage 2 of **C2SPrInDT** were not worse than for DBRT. For English, the balanced accuracy was even slightly better than in DBRT. This shows that the *Exo-approach* is quite competitive, though it does not use the original endogenous variables as predictors for model building as in DBRT. The high balanced accuracies show that the exogenous properties of the signs, like their location, their purpose, and so on, are very suitable to predict which language is displayed on the sign. The REx models at stage 1 already predict more than 80% of the languages correctly. However, the only small difference between the accuracies at stages 1 and 2 indicates that predictions of the appearance of other languages by means of exogenous variables do not improve accuracies very much. At stage 2, the predictions of a language on a sign generated by the stage 1 models are included as additional predictors. These predictors are named English_2S, French_2S, and Dutch_2S, with 2S standing for the second stage. Actually, the predicted language is only included once in the best tree models at stage 2, namely the prediction of English (feature English_2S) in the model for French, as illustrated by the tree in Figure 15. In this tree, location plays the most prominent role for the use of French (indicated in dark gray). French is predicted to be displayed on the sign if the location is Marigot and the only language on the sign is not predicted as English, or if there is more than one language on the sign. For Philipsburg, French is only predicted if the number of languages displayed on the sign is 3 or more (Node 3), or if one or two languages are displayed, the multilingual type is 2, 3, or 4, and the sign is of the type digital, graffiti, road sign, shop window, or sticker (Node 6).

For **SimCPrInDT**, Table 9 shows that the *EndoI-approach* at stage 2 (REnI) has improved the mean balanced accuracy by 13.7% compared to stage 1 and by 8.6% compared to the stage 2 REx analysis. The *EndoJ-approach* (REnJ) generates the same models for Dutch and English as the *EndoI-approach* but a model with a slightly lower balanced accuracy for French. Compared to the DBR variant of **PrInDTMulab**, the Endo approach leads to a slight improvement at stage 2 for the languages French and Dutch.

5.6.2 Simultaneous Regression Models

In Section 4.5.6.3, we mentioned that not only simultaneous classification models can be estimated by the functions **C2SPrInDT** and **SimCPrInDT** (cf. Section 5.6.1) but also simultaneous regression models can be estimated by the functions **R2SPrInDT** and **SimRPrInDT** (two-stage regression by means of the *Exo-* and *Endo-approaches*). The syntax of the functions **R2SPrInDT** and **SimRPrInDT** is very similar to the syntax of the functions **C2SPrInDT** and **SimCPrInDT**. Simultaneous regression modeling was successfully applied to the properties of vowels as introduced in Section 2.1.4. However, because of space restrictions, we will publish the results elsewhere.

5.6.3 Simultaneous Mixed Models

As an application of **Mix2SPrInDT** and **SimMixPrInDT** (two-stage mixed modeling by the *Exo-* and *Endo-approaches*), we discuss the potential interdependence of subject-pronoun realization, past-tense marking, and vowel length (cf. Sections 2.1.1, 2.1.3, and 2.1.4). These analyses are based on three different data sets with different endogenous variables, for which the observed elements of the substructure (i.e., the children) and the predictors used for modeling are not identical and need to be adapted and partly transformed for a joint analysis.

At stage 1 of **Mix2SPrInDT**, the functions **PrInDT** and **PrInDTMulev** are used as in Sections 5.1.1 and 5.3, together with the **PrInDTreg** function, which

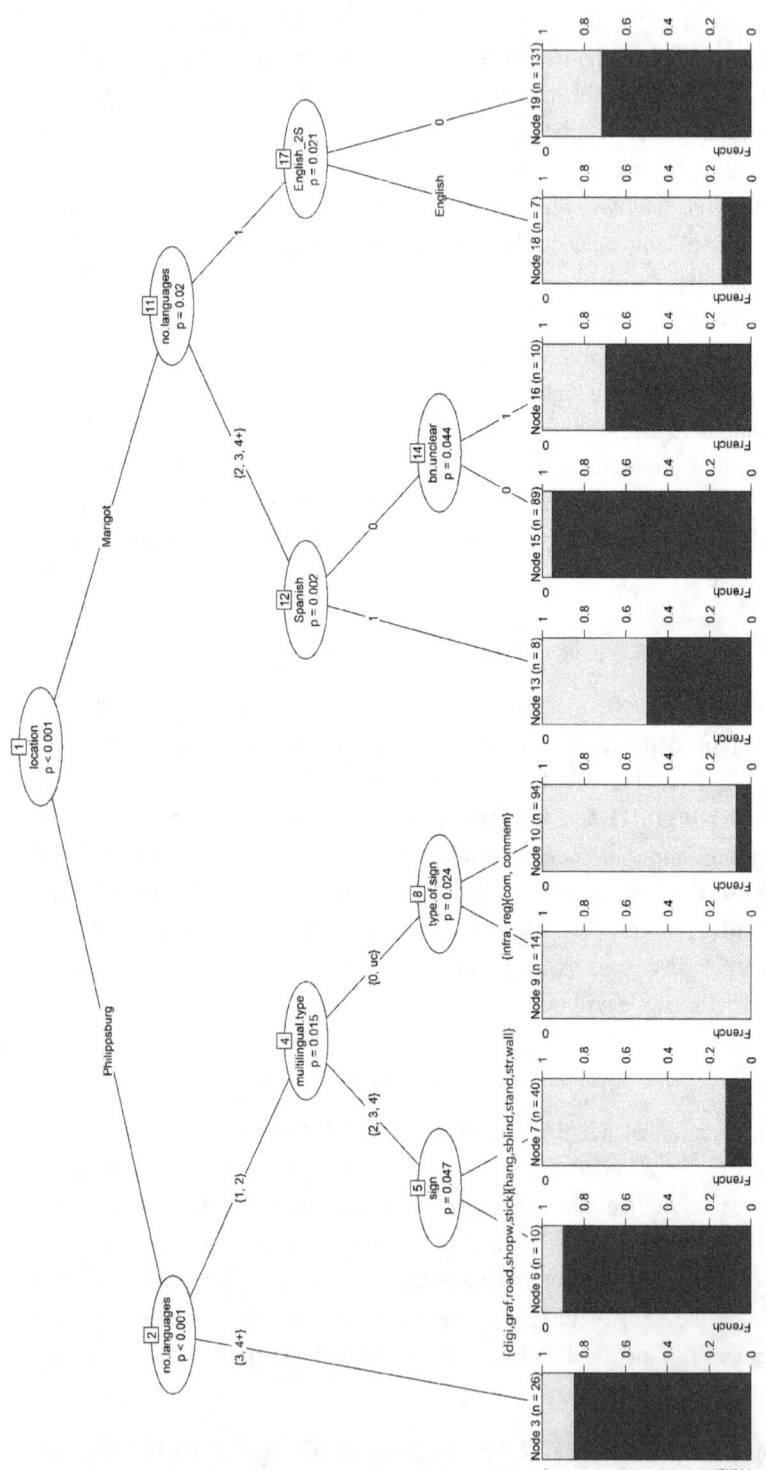

Figure 15 Tree for French: C2SPrInDT stage 2 result.

aims to model vowels lengths (cf. Section 5.4.1). At stage 2, summaries of the predictions of the endogenous variables generated by the stage 1 models are used as additional predictors (cf. Section 4.5.6.3). For example, in the model for subject-pronoun realization, the predictions of the endogenous variables "past-tense marking" and "vowel length" are used. Since the observed elements of the substructure in the different data sets are different, we use summaries of all predictions of the endogenous variables for a child as additional predictors. As summaries per child, the percentages of *zero* and "nonstandard marking" (= *unmarked + finish*) are used for subject-pronoun realization and past-tense marking; for vowel length realization, we use the mean of vowel length. If an endogenous variable is not observed for a child, the mean of the summaries of this endogenous variable calculated from all those children who produced the variable is used as the summary for this child.

For both **Mix2SPrInDT** and **SimMixPrInDT**, all information about the relevant data sets and all inputs for the functions employed to analyze them need to be specified as a first step. The list of data sets (datalist) for which we want to build a simultaneous model is specified by the sublists datanames, targets, datastruc, and summ. The sublist datanames specifies the relevant data sets, the sublist targets the labels of the endogenous variable for each data set. The PrInDT functions utilize the names of the endogenous variables for labeling the predictions of the endogenous variables. Therefore, we renamed the target variables from "real," "class," and "vowel_length" in Sections 2.1.1, 2.1.3, and 2.1.4 to "zero," "past," and "vowel" as short and informative indicators of the contents. The variables representing the children in the different data sets have to be specified in datastruc. For discrete targets, the list summ includes the classes for which we want to calculate the summary percentages; for each continuous target summ is set to NA. For a discrete target, a sublist of classes to be combined can be specified. In our case, sumpast <- paste("unmarked","finish",sep=",") specifies that the percentage of *unmarked+finish* should be calculated for "past." The respective R-code to specify the datalist reads as follows:

```
datanames <- list("datazero","datapast","datavowel")
# data frames of relevant datasets
targets <- c("zero","past","vowel") # targets in the order of datanames
datastruc <- list(CHILDzero,CHILDpast,CHILDvowel) # substructures in the same order
sumpast <- paste("unmarked","finish",sep=",") # sep = separator
summ <- c("zero",sumpast,NA) # classes to build percentages, NA for regression
datalist <- list(datanames=datanames,targets=targets,datastruc=datastruc,
summ=summ)
```

The functions **PrInDT** and **PrInDTreg**, employed to analyze the data sets, use percentages for the large (percl) and the small (percs) classes for discrete targets and percentages for the observations (pobs) and the predictors (ppre) for continuous targets. These percentages can be specified in the matrix percent. Cases in which default percentages should be used, or percentages chosen automatically as for datapast are indicated by NAs. To achieve this automatically, the matrix percent is initialized by NAs. The specification is illustrated in the following R-code for the call of **Mix2SPrInDT**:

```
percent <- matrix(NA,nrow=3,ncol=2) # initialization: 3 rows, 2 columns
percent[1,] <- c("percl=0.075","percs=0.9") # percentages for datazero
percent[3,] <- c("pobs=0.9","ppre=c(0.9,0.8,0.7)") # percentages for datavowel
# datalist as above, ctestv as for subpro
out2SMix <- Mix2SPrInDT(datalist,ctestv,N=999,percent=percent,conf.level=0.99)
```

For **SimMixPrInDT**, interdependence is generated by summaries of the observed endogenous variables instead of summaries of the predicted endogenous variables. At stage 1 of the approach, ctrees are applied to the full data set, including those summaries as additional predictors. At stage 2, version d of structured subsampling (cf. Section 4.5.1) is implemented (i.e., we subsample first from the children according to a substructure Struc and then from the predictors). The substructure is defined as Struc=list(check="ETH",labs=labs). In Struc, the variable name check="ETH" is specified without a data set name since it is different for the different models (cf. Section 5.1.2 for the general specification of Struc). The percentages are used as specified in percent for **Mix2SPrInDT**, except for ppre=c(0.9,0.7,0.5).

At stage 2 of **SimMixPrInDT**, we based our modeling on (nsub=)20 randomly chosen children, each from Singapore and England. For all data sets, at least 20 children are available for both Singapore and England, except for *past*. For the *past* data, we chose 20 children from Singapore and all 19 children available for England. We repeated the random choice of children M=6 times and the random choices of the percentages of the predictors and the observations in ppre and pobs N=333 times for each choice of the children. We used the following R-code:

```
# datalist,ctestv as for Mix2SPrInDT
# percent as for Mix2SPrInDT except for percent[3,] re-specified below
Struc <- list(check="ETH",labs=labs) # labs as for PrInDTCstruc
percent[3,] <- c("pobs=0.9","ppre=c(0.9,0.7,0.5)") # percentages for datavowel
outSimMix <- SimMixPrInDT(datalist,ctestv,Struc=Struc,M=6,N=333,nsub=20,
percent=percent,conf.level=0.99)
```

Optimizing Decision Trees for the Analysis of World Englishes　85

Table 10 Accuracies of the joint two-stage analysis of classification and regression trees

Variable	REx1	REx2	REn1	REnI	REnJ
pronoun	0.7046500	**0.7064300**	0.5000000	0.7033261	0.6887827
past	**0.6783925**	0.6687240	0.6123175	0.6715204	0.5200236
vowel	0.5043433	0.5056695	0.3933240	**0.5122668**	0.4596022

Considering the results of **Mix2SPrInDT** (cf. REx1 and REx2 in Table 10), we can see that the stage 1 models already show quite high accuracies (0.70, 0.68, 0.5). The improvements at stage 2 are rather small. For the *past* data set, we generated three trees, one for each of the classes *marked*, *unmarked*, and *finish*. Each of these trees has its individual balanced accuracy. At stage 1, they are 0.786, 0.778, and 0.831 (the same as for **PrInDTMulev** in Section 5.3). At stage 2, the balanced accuracies of the corresponding trees are 0.784, 0.785, and 0.835, respectively. Figure 16 illustrates the tree for the class *finish* at stage 2. The balanced accuracy of this tree is slightly higher than for the tree at stage 1. The tree has a very similar structure as the stage 1 result (cf. Figure 9), but one of its splits employs the prediction of vowel_length ("pvowel"). Comparing the trees at stages 1 and 2, it appears that for LiBa = {*bili1*,*multi2*}, the following two properties are equally good indicators for the class *finish*: "high (predicted) vowel lengths" and "verb is not of high frequency" (cf. Figure 9). This is in line with earlier research – for example, Tomaschek et al. (2013), who point out that "in English, HF (high frequency) words have been shown to contain more centralized and shorter vowels than LF (low frequency) words."

As Table 10 illustrates, the accuracies gained by REnI of **SimMixPrInDT** are similar to those in REx2. Therefore, in REnI the additional information from the other endogenous variables does not really improve the accuracy of the models. Only for vowel length does REnI gain an improvement over REx, and the R^2 of the best tree (0.5123) is only somewhat lower than the overall best R^2 found by **PrInDTRstruc** (0.5158). The best tree does not include the summaries of the other endogenous variables (cf. Figure 17) and has the same structure but not the same split values as the best tree found by **PrInDTreg** (cf. Figure 10). The best trees for pronoun realization and past-tense marking are not illustrated here since their balanced accuracies are even lower than for REx.

For the REnJ approach, we first identified the 38 children for which all three endogenous variables are observed (i.e., 19 from Singapore and 19 from England). Then, we repeated model construction at stage 2, based on these 38 children only. The result is presented in the last column of Table 10. Since

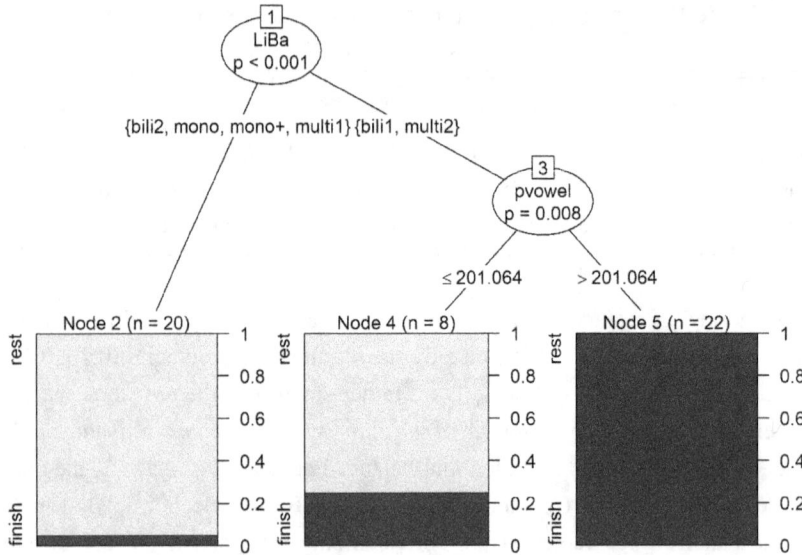

Figure 16 Best REx2 classification tree for the class "finish."

accuracy loss was considerably small for only subject-pronoun realization (cf. the last two columns of Table 10), a competitive model was built just for this case. Overall, the restriction to those children for which all endogenous variables were observed appears to generate such a loss in accuracy that the resulting models are not interesting for further discussion.

5.7 Summary: Selection Criteria of PrInDT Functions and Best Models

In this Element, we discussed a number of different methods for modeling and optimizing decision trees. For further instruction on how to use the various PrInDT functions, we summarize the most important aspects for selection and application in Table 11.

Let us, finally, discuss the best models generated by the various PrInDT methods in Sections 5.1–5.6. We analyzed our World Englishes data sets by means of different PrInDT functions employing individual or simultaneous modeling of endogenous variables (single equation and interdependent models) – that is, in some functions endogenous variables are employed as predictors and in other functions they are not. In the following, we will summarize the accuracies of the best models identified for our data sets and their respective PrInDT functions.

For subject-pronoun realization, the overall best tree with a balanced accuracy of 0.7059 is generated by structured subsampling (**PrInDTCstruc**; cf.

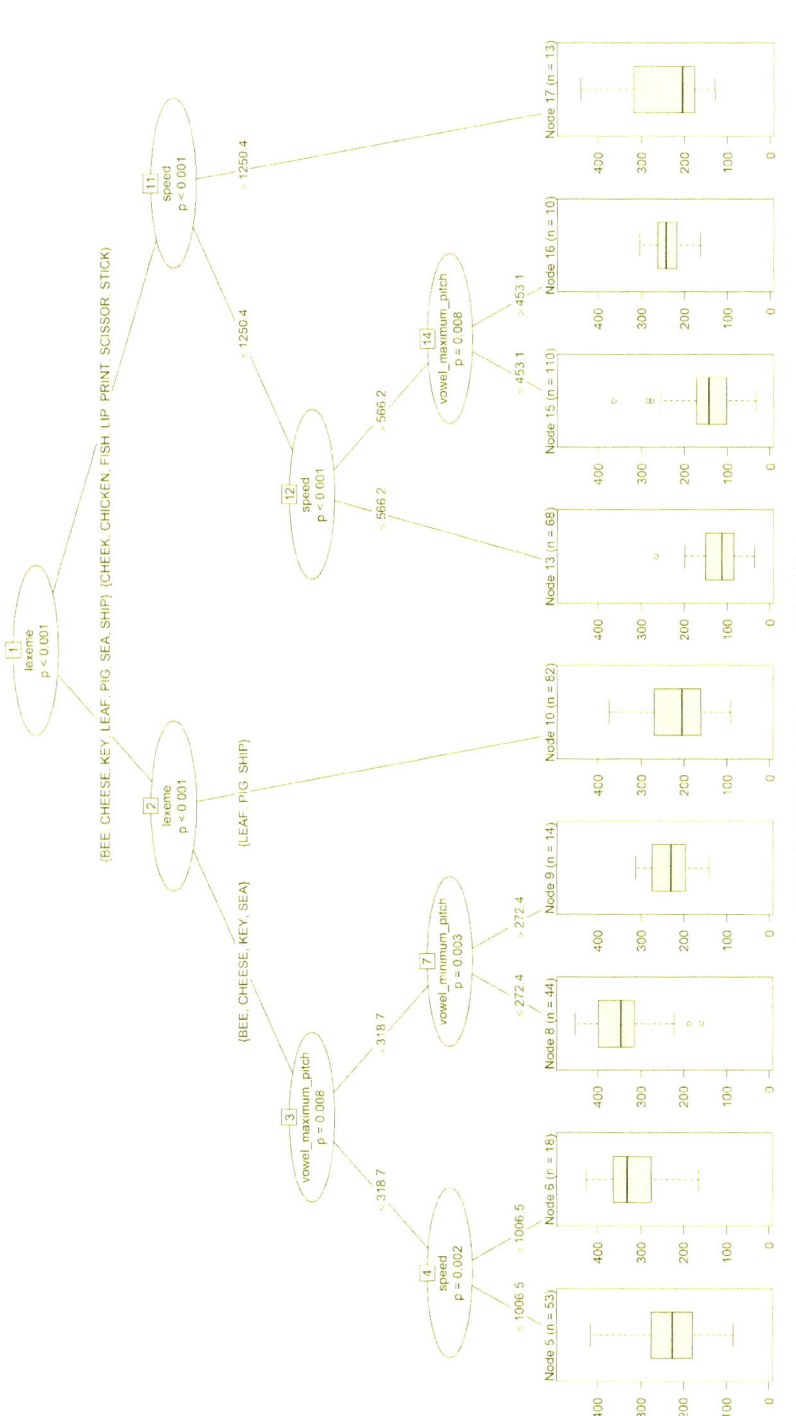

Figure 17 Best tree for *vowel* in REnI.

Table 11 Advice for the application of PrInDT for the different targets

a) Classification	PrInDT function	Categorical target(s)
2-class	**PrInDT** **RePrInDT** **OptPrInDT** **PrInDTCstruc**	If your target has two classes, start with the standard method **PrInDT** and its default class percentages. You can try out your own percentages either with **PrInDT** (one percentage per class) or with **RePrInDT** (lists of possible percentages per class). You can optimize the class percentages with **OptPrInDT** by simply specifying the largest percentages and their distances to their immediate lower ones. If you intend to interpret the random selection of observations generated by subsampling for the best model, then employ **PrInDTCstruc**. You can compare the results of four different versions of this function.
2-class and unbalanced predictor	**NesPrInDT**	If your target has two classes and your data includes one predictor with unbalanced classes, use **NesPrInDT**.
Multi-class	**PrInDTMulev**	If your target has more than two classes, use **PrInDTMulev**.
Multi-label	**PrInDTMulab** **C2SPrInDT** **SimCPrInDT**	If you want to consider more than one categorical target (here called label) jointly, you can employ the function **PrInDTMulab**, which includes both modeling with exogenous predictors only as well as with endogenous predictors. Alternatively, you can employ the function **C2SPrInDT** for only modeling with exogenous predictors and the extended function **SimCPrInDT** for exogenous and endogenous predictors.

Table 11 (cont.)

b) Regression		Continuous target(s)
One target	**PrInDTreg** **PrInDTRstruc**	PrInDTreg is the standard method for one continuous target. If you intend to interpret a random selection of observations for the best model, then employ **PrInDTRstruc**. You can compare the results of four different versions of this function.
More than one target	**R2SPrInDT** **SimRPrInDT**	If you want to consider more than one continuous target jointly, employ **R2SPrInDT** for modeling with only exogenous predictors and **SimRPrInDT** for modeling with exogenous and endogenous predictors.
c) Mixed modeling		**Categorical and continuous targets**
More than one target	**Mix2SPrInDT** **SimMixPrInDT**	If you want to consider categorical and continuous targets jointly, employ **Mix2SPrInDT** for modeling with only exogenous predictors and **SimMixPrInDT** for modeling with exogenous and endogenous predictors.

Section 5.1.2). In the study with unbalanced predictors, only one PrInDT function (**NesPrInDT**) was applied. The best balanced accuracy was 0.57 (cf. Section 5.2). For past-tense markings, by modeling with **PrInDTMulev** the prediction of the smallest class *finish* is close to perfect (92% accuracy), and the overall balanced accuracy is 0.68 (cf. Section 5.3). For vowel lengths, the overall best outcome of the PrInDT functions is generated by structured resampling with an $R^2 = 0.52$ (**PrInDTRstruc**; cf. Section 5.4.3). For the St. Martin landscaping study, the languages French, Dutch, and English are already very well predicted by the exogenous characteristics of the signs with balanced accuracies between 82% and 89% (**PrInDTMulab**; cf. Section 5.5; **C2SPrInDT**; cf. Section 5.6.1). If the other languages are allowed as predictors,

the balanced accuracies for all three languages are higher than 90%, even up to 96% (**SimCPrInDT**; cf. Section 5.6.1).

6 Achievements for World Englishes Studies

In the following section, we reflect on and summarize the achievements our approaches offer for analyzing linguistic variation in the study of World Englishes.

First of all – and as already argued in Section 3.2.3.3 – we point out again that, in general, decision trees are easy and straightforward to interpret, even for beginners in statistics. Decision trees are based on a series of so-called if-then rules, which makes them very accessible for human understanding (cf. our interpretation of trees in Section 5).

Decision trees automatically model interactions of predictors (cf. Sections 3.2.3.3 and 5.4.2), which distinctly reduces model complexity. For linear models, interactions have to be explicitly included in the list of predictors (cf. Section 3.2.3.1), which makes them even more complex to interpret.

If decision trees include splits that contradict expectations based on earlier and often long-standing and empirically tested linguistic assumptions, they can be easily restricted for better interpretation (cf. Section 4.2 and Sections 5.1, 5.3, 5.4, and 5.6). This is because splits rely on individual variables.

Easy interpretation is one of the main advantages of decision trees. Unfortunately, this advantage is lost for large trees. Therefore, we have suggested restricting trees in size by adjusting the respective significance level and introduced a way to optimize the accuracy of those trees by means of subsampling. We argue that model accuracy alone is not decisive but that trees need to be linguistically interpretable (cf. Section 4.2) and that in a number of randomly generated trees, some of them might, by chance, go against earlier theoretical assumptions and/or mistakenly against one's own expectations. This is why we argue that our analysis should never rely on the first and one tree only but that a series of models should be generated via subsampling and investigated concerning interpretability and accuracy (cf. Section 4.3). Therefore, for model selection, both interpretability and accuracy should be considered and weighed against each other (cf. Section 4.1). To keep our models simple, we decided to put more weight on interpretability and optimize model accuracy for a restricted model size (cf. Section 5.4.2 for an example of the comparison of different kinds of models).

By comparing many trees, decision trees generated by one of the various PrInDT approaches (cf. Sections 4.5 and 5) are able to identify the split variable and the corresponding split value(s) that best separate the classes or the

Table 12 Root splits

Study	Cf. sections	Root split in	Comments
subject pronoun realization	5.1	PRN, i.e., the subject pronoun itself (intralinguistic)	The pronoun *it* was identified to behave differently from the other pronouns, in that it is more frequently left out (i.e., *zero*).
unbalanced predictor	5.2	PRN (intralinguistic)	Again, PRN is the first split dividing the data into *it* versus all other pronouns.
past-tense marking	5.3, 5.6.3	LiBa (extralinguistic)	Linguistic background plays the most important role.
vowel length	5.4	lexeme (intralinguistic)	The vowel length of some lexemes, namely *pig*, *ship*, and *cheek*, is not realized as expected for "standard" English.
linguistic landscaping	5.5, 5.6.1	location or number of languages on the sign (extralinguistic)	Location splits data into Marigot and Philipsburg and thus has a significant influence on the prediction of languages on signs. 'No. of languages on the sign' distinguishes one language versus more than one.

distributions of the continuous target in the subnodes. This variable builds the "root split" of the best tree (i.e., its first split) and is decisive for the interpretation of the relationship between target and predictors. Table 12 shows the root split variables, identified by PrInDT, and their interpretation.

As mentioned as part of the discussion of model accuracy and unbalanced data sets, regular decision trees trained on the full sample are often not ideally suited for variationist/sociolinguistic analyses. They can, however, be optimized by means of resampling as exemplified in a number of the PrInDT approaches introduced previously. In terms of the choice of an adequate accuracy criterion for optimizing classification trees, measuring balanced accuracies guarantees that the best model also predicts the smaller class in variationist approaches that are characterized by a very unequal distribution of classes. In Section 1, we have argued that models which have a high overall accuracy but never or insufficiently predict the smaller class are inacceptable, in particular since the smaller class is normally the focus of interest for a study investigating linguistic variation. Such inadequate models often result from modeling imbalanced classes based on the full sample since then the larger class dominates the analysis. An example is discussed in Section 3.2.4. By means of undersampling and the use of balanced accuracy as an optimization criterion, our PrInDT approach generates models that also predict sufficient numbers of observations of the smaller class (cf. Section 5.1).

In classification, we use the balanced accuracy as a quality measure (in regression, the standard R^2). Model construction is carried out on subsamples; model evaluation by our quality measures, however, is carried out on the full sample to make the results of the different subsamples comparable. Overall, with our PrInDT approach, we constructed models with a distinctly higher quality than the models constructed on the full sample (cf. Table 13). This is only possible since standard decision trees are trained to optimize the decisions for each individual split and not to produce optimal accuracy on the training sample. Therefore, we rely on many repetitions of tree construction on subsamples and take the tree with the best accuracy on the full sample. By means of our PrInDT approach, we identified the highest improvements for those classification analyses for which the data set showed the highest imbalance between the classes (cf. first and last line in Table 13). This supports our PrInDT idea of undersampling. The R^2 of the regression tree for vowel length is also strongly increased by 31% by our subsampling procedure. These two findings reinforce

Table 13 Balanced accuracies (ba) or R^2s for models based on the full sample and PrInDT

Topic	Measure	Full sample	PrInDT	% improved
Subject pronoun	ba	**0.500**	**0.708**	**42**
Speaker imbalance	ba	0.515	0.574	11
Past tense	ba	0.612	0.678	11
Vowel length	R^2	0.393	0.516	**31**
Three languages	ba (mean)	0.820	0.933	14
Language Dutch	ba (BR)	**0.600**	**0.870**	**45**

our observation that decision trees based on the full sample often do not produce satisfactory results and stress the value and functionality of PrInDT.

In addition, structured resampling can improve model interpretation and even model quality in two ways. First of all, it helps identify the most representative participants of a study, which best cover the overall variation generated by the children. Secondly, it also helps determine the most important predictors for model building. For example, the best model we found for subject-pronoun realization (cf. Section 5.1.2) was generated by structured resampling with the function **PrInDTCstruc** version d (cf. Figure 7) – that is by first subsampling from the children and then from the predictors (with additional undersampling). This model is only based on 20 children each from Singapore and England (40 children out of 51 overall) and on the 4 predictors PRN, ETH, AGE, and SEX (predictors MLU and LiBa not used). For vowel length prediction, the best model was also generated by structured resampling (cf. Figure 12).

Next to the optimization and modification of decision trees in terms of accuracy, interpretability, and re-/undersampling, we have also introduced PrInDT versions that are able to model multiclass problems. This was done by means one-versus-rest modeling, which has the advantage that we first analyze differences between each of the individual classes and the other classes and then combine the resulting models to assess the multiclass situation. Therefore, we can compare two-class accuracies with multiclass ones. For past-tense marking (cf. Section 2.1.3), **PrInDTMulev** demonstrates that the balanced accuracy of the two-class task *marked* versus *nonstandard* (*finish* plus *unmarked*) is much higher (0.79) than for the three-class variant (0.68; cf. Section 5.3).

As a next step, we introduced the idea of endogenous and exogenous variables and how they relate to each other. Simultaneous modeling that is only based on exogenous variables (i.e., where endogenous variables are avoided as predictors) may already lead to acceptable models (which we call the *Exo-approach*). In this respect, we demonstrated that the two-stage *Exo-approach* in **C2SPrInDT** aptly emulates the three-stage DBRT approach from **PrInDTMulab** (cf. Section 5.5). In DBRT, an estimation by means of the endogenous predictors is employed, though only the dependence on the exogenous variables is of interest. This detour via the use of the endogenous variables is avoided in **C2SPrInDT**, with an even somewhat better result (cf. Section 5.6.1).

Last but not least, we discuss an aspect of our results that relates to World Englishes model building and interpretation in general. Sociolinguistic variables are essential to account for heterogeneity in linguistic data and their results. Even though this may appear to be clear and a fundamental prerequisite of a linguistic study for the sociolinguist, studies of large corpora, heavily influenced by inferential statistics, often ignore these parameters or cannot take them into consideration since, in particular, older corpora or internet-based collections of linguistic materials do not contain the relevant speaker information. This often obstructs necessary contextualization and thus full interpretability of results. For example, in our comparison of pronoun realization by Singaporean children and adults (cf. Sections 2.1.2 and 5.2), we observed that the adults appear to be very heterogeneous in their pronoun realization. Unfortunately, no additional sociolinguistic information is available from the ICE-Singapore, which would help explain this heterogeneity. This is, of course, problematic for any kind of analysis, and we would therefore like to raise a word of caution against the current big data craze prevalent in many linguistic fields. Of course, large databases offer invaluable repositories for analyses, but not when they come at the expense of general interpretability and contextualization due to missing sociolinguistic information. In this respect, smaller, well-annotated corpora, like the ones presented in this Element, might come with the same if not higher linguistic value than the big data currently propagated. In the end, it should be kept in mind that this is what statistics was invented for: to analyze even small data sets in ways that make them more representative.

7 Conclusion

In this Element, we presented our PrInDT approach and applied it to selected World Englishes data sets, collected by the first author of the Element. Some of the new statistical methods were published in earlier papers; some have been discussed in this Element for the first time.

Overall, our PrInDT approach clearly improved model building and our understanding of the World Englishes studies, which the methods have been applied to. We have focused on accuracy and interpretability, two aspects of model building that are equally relevant for sophisticated modeling, and the interpretation of linguistic data (and probably any kind of data), and have shown how both can be improved in various types of data (for further details on the main achievements of PrInDT for World Englishes studies, cf. Section 6).

Finally, we would like to indicate some brief ideas for further work. In this Element, for reasons of space, we had to limit our presentation to the use of some of the PrInDT functions. Many other PrInDT functions exist that could be applied to the introduced data and, of course, further data sets. In the PrInDT software package, a variety of further functions exist. For an overview of these, you can call up the following help function:

```
help(package=PrInDT)
```

In this Element we put a particular focus on the best model for interpretation. Sometimes, however, the accuracies of the best, second-best, and third-best models are nearly identical. Therefore, generally, PrInDT can identify the two or three best models so that they can also be considered for interpretation. We can also calculate the accuracy of ensembles of the three best models for a comparison with the best accuracy of a single model in PrInDT (cf. Weihs & Buschfeld 2021a for a discussion).

Moreover, because of space restrictions, we did not report on simultaneous regression models (i.e., on the PrInDT functions R2SPrInDT and SimRPrInDT). Moreover, the development of PrInDT is ongoing. In particular, more structured sampling options are planned to be implemented in simultaneous modeling.

Last but not least, in this Element we introduced a successful application of simultaneous modeling of linguistic characteristics, in our case pronoun realization, past-tense marking, and vowel length. This means of considering dependencies of variables may be worthwhile to pursue in the development of further statistical methods since such dependencies are underresearched in the World Englishes paradigm, and certainly also in other subdisciplines of linguistics, but might add relevant, maybe even eye-opening, new findings to even long-studied varieties of English.

References

Angelino, Elaine, Nicholas Larus-Stone, Daniel Alabi, Margo Seltzer, & Cynthia Rudin. 2018. Learning certifiably optimal rule lists for categorical data. *Journal of Machine Learning Research* 18: 1–78. https://doi.org/10.48550/arXiv.1704.01701.

Baayen, R. Harald. 2008. *Analyzing Linguistic Data: A Practical Introduction to Statistics Using R*. Cambridge: Cambridge University Press.

Backhaus, Peter. 2006. Multilingualism in Tokyo: A look into the linguistic landscape. *International Journal of Multilingualism* 3(1): 52–66. https://doi.org/10.1080/14790710608668385.

Boersma, Paul, & David Weenink. 2018. *Praat: Doing Phonetics by Computer (Version 6.0.37)*. www.praat.org. Accessed July 29, 2023.

Buschfeld, Sarah. 2020. *Children's English in Singapore: Acquisition, Properties, and Use*. London: Routledge. https://doi.org/10.4324/9781315201030.

Buschfeld, Sarah, Sven Leuckert, Claus Weihs, & Andreas Weilinghoff. 2024. How real is the quantitative turn? Investigating statistics as the new normal in linguistics. *ICAME Journal* 48(1): 1–22. https://doi.org/10.2478/icame-2024-0001.

Buschfeld, Sarah, & Claus Weihs. 2024. Statistical modeling of current linguistic realities around the world: The case of Singapore. In Claus Weihs, Walter Krämer, & Sarah Buschfeld (eds.), *Statistics Today...* Heidelberg: Springer Berlin, 213–223. https://doi.org/10.1007/978-3-662-68907-3.

Buschfeld, Sarah, Claus Weihs, & Patricia Ronan. 2024. Modeling linguistic landscapes: A comparison of St Martin's two capitals Philipsburg and Marigot. *Linguistic Landscape* 10(3): 302–334. https://doi.org/10.1075/ll.23070.bus.

Chan, Margaret. 2020. English, mother tongue and the Singapore identity. *The Straits Times*. January 2, 2020. www.straitstimes.com/opinion/english-mother-tongue-and-the-spore-identity. Accessed August 15, 2020.

Department of Statistics Singapore. 2020. *Census of Population 2020, Statistical Release 1: Demographic Characteristics, Education, Language and Religion*. www.singstat.gov.sg/publications/reference/cop2020/cop2020-sr1. Accessed May 28, 2023.

Efron, Bradley. 1979. Bootstrap methods: Another look at the jackknife. *The Annals of Statistics* 7(1): 1–26. https://doi.org/10.1214/aos/1176344552.

Fernando, Jason. 2024. R-squared: Definition, calculation, and interpretation. www.investopedia.com/terms/r/r-squared.asp. Accessed May 31, 2025.

Field, Andy, Jeremy Miles, & Zoé Field. 2012. *Discovering Statistics Using R*. Thousand Oaks, CA: SAGE Publications.

Gries, Stefan Th. 2020. On classification trees and random forests in corpus linguistics: Some words of caution and suggestions for improvement. *Corpus Linguistics and Linguistic Theory* 16(3): 617–647. https://doi.org/10.1515/cllt-2018-0078.

Gries, Stefan Th. 2021. *Statistics for Linguists with R: A Practical Introduction*, 3rd ed. Berlin: De Gruyter Mouton. https://doi.org/10.1515/9783110718256.

Gries, Stefan Th. 2022. MuPDAR for corpus-based learner and variety studies: Two (more) suggestions for improvement. In Susanne Flach & Martin Hilpert (eds.), *Broadening the Spectrum of Corpus Linguistics: New Approaches to Variability and Change*. Amsterdam: John Benjamins, 257–283. https://doi.org/10.1075/scl.105.09gri.

Grubinger, Thomas, Achim Zeileis, & Karl-Peter Pfeiffer. 2014. evtree: Evolutionary learning of globally optimal classification and regression trees in R. *Journal of Statistical Software* 61(1): 1–29. https://doi.org/10.18637/jss.v061.i01.

Halliday, Michael Alexander Kirkwood, & Ruqaiya Hasan. 1976. *Cohesion in English*. London: Longman. https://doi.org/10.4324/9781315836010.

Hastie, Trevor, Robert Tibshirani, & Jerome Friedman. 2008. *The Elements of Statistical Learning*, 2nd ed. New York: Springer. https://doi.org/10.1007/978-0-387-84858-7.

Ho, Tin Kam. 1998. The random subspace method for constructing decision forests. *IEEE Transactions on Pattern Analysis and Machine Intelligence* 20(8): 832–844. https://doi.org/10.1109/34.709601.

Hothorn, Torsten, Kurt Hornik, & Achim Zeileis. 2006. Unbiased recursive partitioning: A conditional inference framework. *Journal of Computational and Graphical Statistics* 15(3): 651–674. https://doi.org/10.1198/106186006X133933.

ICE-Singapore. *International Corpus of English*. www.ice-corpora.uzh.ch/en/joinice/Teams/icesin.html. Accessed September 1, 2022.

Kortmann, Bernd, Kate Burridge, Rajend Mesthri, Edgar W. Schneider, & Clive Upton (eds.). 2004. *A Handbook of Varieties of English, Vol. II: Morphology and Syntax*. Berlin: Mouton de Gruyter.

Kortmann, Bernd, Kerstin Lunkenheimer, & Katharina Ehret (eds.). 2020. *The Electronic World Atlas of Varieties of English*. Zenodo. http://ewave-atlas.org. Accessed September 25, 2022. https://doi.org/10.5281/zenodo.3712132.

Kwan-Terry, Anna. 1986. The acquisition of word order in English and Cantonese interrogative sentences: A Singapore case study. *RELC Journal* 17(1): 14–39. https://doi.org/10.1177/003368828601700102.

Laabs, Björn-Hergen, Ana Westenberger, & Inke R. König. 2024. Identification of representative trees in random forests based on a new tree-based distance measure. *Advances in Data Analysis and Classification* 18: 363–380. https://doi.org/10.1007/s11634-023-00537-7.

Lachenbruch, Peter A., & M. Ray Mickey. 1968. Estimation of error rates in discriminant analysis. *Technometrics* 10(1): 1–11. https://doi.org/10.1080/00401706.1968.10490530.

Larsson, Tove, Luke Plonsky, & Gregory R. Hancock. 2021. On the benefits of structural equation modeling for corpus linguists. *Corpus Linguistics and Linguistic Theory* 17(3): 683–714. https://doi.org/10.1515/cllt-2020-0051.

Levshina, Natalia. 2015. *How to Do Linguistics with R: Data Exploration and Statistical Analysis*. Amsterdam: John Benjamins. https://doi.org/10.1075/z.195.website.

Levshina, Natalia. 2022. Comparing Bayesian and frequentist models of language variation. In Ole Schützler & Julia Schlüter (eds.), *Data and Methods in Corpus Linguistics: Comparative Approaches*... Cambridge: Cambridge University Press, 224–258. https://doi.org/10.1017/9781108589314.009.

Lüdecke, Daniel. 2024. *sjPlot: Data Visualization for Statistics in Social Science (R Package Version 2.8.17)*. https://cran.r-project.org/web/packages/sjPlot/index.html. Accessed June 23, 2025.

Politis, Dimitris N., Joseph P. Romano, & Michael Wolf. 1999. *Subsampling*. New York: Springer. https://doi.org/10.1007/978-1-4612-1554-7.

Probst, Philipp, Quay Au, Giuseppe Casalicchio, Clemens Stachl, & Bernd Bischl. 2017. Multilabel classification with R package mlr. *The R Journal* 9(1): 352–369. https://doi.org/10.32614/RJ-2017-012.

Rasinger, Sebastian M. 2013. *Quantitative Research in Linguistics: An Introduction*, 2nd ed. London: Bloomsbury Academic. https://doi.org/10.5040/9781350284883.

R Core Team. 2019. *R: A Language and Environment for Statistical Computing*. Vienna: R Foundation for Statistical Computing. www.R-project.org.

Rice, Mabel L., & Kenneth Wexler. 2001. *Rice/Wexler Test of Early Grammatical Impairment: Examiner's Manual*. San Antonio: The Psychological Corporation.

Rissanen, Jorma. 1978. Modeling by shortest data description. *Automatica* 14(5): 465–471. https://doi.org/10.1016/0005-1098(78)90005-5.

Roeper, Thomas, & Bernhard Rohrbacher. 2000. Null subjects in early child language and the economy of projection. In Susan M. Powers &

Cornelia Hamann (eds.), *Acquisition of Scrambling and Cliticization*. Berlin: Springer, 345–396. https://doi.org/10.1007/978-94-017-3232-1_14.

Rosseel, Yves. 2012. lavaan: An R package for structural equation modeling. *Journal of Statistical Software* 48(2): 1–36. https://doi.org/10.18637/jss.v048.i02.

Schneider, Edgar W., Kate Burridge, Bernd Kortmann, Rajend Mesthrie, & Clive Upton. 2004. *A Handbook of Varieties of English, Vol. 1: Phonology*. Berlin: Mouton de Gruyter. https://doi.org/10.1515/9783110197181.

Schneider, Gerold, & Max Lauber. 2019. *Statistics for Linguists: A Patient, Slow-Paced Introduction to Statistics and to the Programming Language R*. Digitale Lehre und Forschung UZH. https://dlf.uzh.ch/openbooks/statisticsforlinguists . Accessed September 1, 2022.

Sonderegger, Morgan. 2023. *Regression Modeling for Linguistic Data*. Cambridge: MIT Press. https://doi.org/10.17605/OSF.IO/PNUMG.

Strobl, Carolin, Yannick Rothacher, Sven Theiler, & Mirka Henninger. 2024. Detecting interactions with random forests: A comment on Gries' words of caution and suggestions for improvement. *Corpus Linguistics and Linguistic Theory*. https://doi.org/10.1515/cllt-2024-0028.

Tagliamonte, Sali A., & Harald R. Baayen. 2012. Models, forests, and trees of York English: Was/were variation as a case study for statistical practice. *Language Variation and Change* 24(2): 135–178. https://doi.org/10.1017/S0954394512000129.

Theil, Henri. 1971. *Principles of Econometrics*. New York: Wiley.

Tibshirani, Robert, & Keith Knight. 1999. Model search by bootstrap "bumping." *Journal of Computational and Graphical Statistics* 8(4): 671–686. https://doi.org/10.2307/1390820.

Tomaschek, Fabian, Martijn Wieling, Denis Arnold, & Harald Baayen. 2013. Word frequency, vowel length and vowel quality in speech production: An EMA study of the importance of experience. In Frédéric Bimbot, Christophe Cerisara, Cécile Fougeron, Guillaume Gravier, Lori Lamel, François Pellegrino, & Pascal Perrier (eds.), *The Fourteenth Annual Conference of the International Speech Communication Association (INTERSPEECH 2013)*. International Speech Communications Association, 1302–1306. https://doi.org/10.21437/Interspeech.2013.

Valian, Virginia. 2016. Null subjects. In Jeffrey Lidz, William Snyder, & Joe Pater (eds.), *The Oxford Handbook of Developmental Linguistics*. Oxford: Oxford University Press, 386–413. https://doi.org/10.1093/oxfordhb/9780199601264.013.17.

Wee, Lionel. 2004. Singapore English: Phonology. In Edgar W. Schneider, Kate Burridge, Bernd Kortmann, Rajend Mesthrie, & Clive Upton (eds.),

A Handbook of Varieties of English: Volume 1: Phonology. Berlin: Mouton de Gruyter, 1017–1033. https://doi.org/10.1515/9783110197181-066.

Weihs, Claus, & Sarah Buschfeld. 2021a. *Combining Prediction and Interpretation in Decision Trees (PrInDT): A Linguistic Example*. https://doi.org/10.48550/arXiv.2103.02336.

Weihs, Claus, & Sarah Buschfeld. 2021b. *NesPrInDT: Nested Undersampling in PrInDT*. https://doi.org/10.48550/arXiv.2103.14931.

Weihs, Claus, & Sarah Buschfeld. 2021c. *Repeated Undersampling in PrInDT (RePrInDT): Variation in Undersampling and Prediction, and Ranking of Predictors in Ensembles*. https://doi.org/10.48550/arXiv.2108.05129.

Weihs, Claus, & Sarah Buschfeld. 2025. *PrInDT: Prediction and Interpretation in Decision Trees for Classification and Regression (R Package Version 2)*. https://doi.org/10.32614/CRAN.package.PrInDT.

Wells, John C. 1982. *Accents of English: An Introduction*. Cambridge: Cambridge University Press.

Winter, Bodo. 2020. *Statistics for Linguists: An Introduction Using R*. New York: Routledge. https://doi.org/10.4324/9781315165547.

Winter, Bodo, & Paul-Christian Bürkner. 2021. Poisson regression for linguists: A tutorial introduction to modelling count data with brms. *Language and Linguistics Compass* 15(11): e12439. https://doi.org/10.1111/lnc3.12439.

Ziegler, Evelyn, Ulrich Schmitz, & Haci-Halil Uslucan. 2018. Attitudes towards visual multilingualism in the linguistic landscape of the Ruhr Area. In Martin Pütz, & Neele Mundt (eds.), *Expanding the Linguistic Landscape*, Amsterdam: John Benjamins, 264–299. https://doi.org/10.21832/9781788922166-015.

World Englishes

Edgar W. Schneider
University of Regensburg

Edgar W. Schneider is Professor Emeritus of English Linguistics at the University of Regensburg, Germany. His many books include *Postcolonial English* (Cambridge, 2007), *English around the World, 2e* (Cambridge, 2020) and *The Cambridge Handbook of World Englishes* (Cambridge, 2020).

Editorial Board

Alexandra D'Arcy, *University of Victoria*
Kate Burridge, *Monash University*
Paul Kerswill, *University of York*
Christian Mair, *University of Freiburg*
Christiane Meierkord, *Ruhr University*
Raj Mesthrie, *University of Cape Town*
Miriam Meyerhoff, *Victoria University of Wellington*
Daniel Schreier, *University of Zurich*
Devyani Sharma, *Queen Mary University of London*
Sali Tagliamonte, *University of Toronto*
Bertus van Rooy, *University of Amsterdam*
Lionel Wee, *National University of Singapore*

About the Series

Over the last centuries, the English language has spread all over the globe due to a multitude of factors including colonization and globalization. In investigating these phenomena, the vibrant linguistic sub-discipline of "World Englishes" has grown substantially, developing appropriate theoretical frameworks and considering applied issues. This Elements series will cover all the topics of the discipline in an accessible fashion and will be supplemented by on-line material.

Cambridge Elements

World Englishes

Elements in the Series

Uniformity and Variability in the Indian English Accent
Caroline R. Wiltshire

Posthumanist World Englishes
Lionel Wee

The Cognitive Foundation of Post-colonial Englishes: Construction Grammar as the Cognitive Theory for the Dynamic Model
Thomas Hoffmann

Inheritance and Innovation in the Evolution of Rural African American English
Guy Bailey, Patricia Cukor-Avila and Juan Salinas

Indian Englishes in the Twenty-First Century: Unity and Diversity in Lexicon and Morphosyntax
Sven Leuckert, Claudia Lange, Tobias Bernaisch and Asya Yurchenko

Language Ideologies and Identities on Facebook and TikTok: A Southern Caribbean Perspective
Guyanne Wilson

Transnational Korean Englishes
Sofia Rüdiger and Alex Baratta

Multiscriptal English in Transliterated Linguistic Landscapes
Chonglong Gu

World Englishes as Components of a Complex Dynamic System
Edgar W. Schneider

Optimizing Decision Trees for the Analysis of World Englishes and Sociolinguistic Data
Sarah Buschfeld and Claus Weihs

A full series listing is available at: www.cambridge.org/EIWE

For EU product safety concerns, contact us at Calle de José Abascal, 56–1°, 28003 Madrid, Spain or eugpsr@cambridge.org.